CAREERS

F O R

CRAFTY
PEOPLE

& Other
Dexterous Types

VGM Careers for You Series

CAREERS FOR CRAFTY PEOPLE

& Other Dexterous Types

Mark Rowh

VGM Career Horizons
a division of *NTC Publishing Group*
Lincolnwood, Illinois USA

Library of Congress Cataloging-in-Publication Data

Rowh, Mark.
   Careers for crafty people and other dexterous types / Mark Rowh.
     p. cm.
   Includes bibliographical references.
   ISBN 0-8442-4106-7 (hard). — ISBN 0-8442-4107-5 (soft)
   1. Handicraft—Vocational guidance—United States. I. Title.
   TT149.R68 1993
   745′.023′73—dc20   93-16030
                                                    CIP

1997 Printing

Published by VGM Career Horizons, a division of NTC Publishing Group.
© 1994 by NTC Publishing Group, 4255 West Touhy Avenue,
Lincolnwood (Chicago), Illinois 60646-1975 U.S.A.

   6 7 8 9 0 VP 9 8 7 6 5 4 3

Dedication

This book is dedicated to all my friends at
New York River Community College.

Contents

About the Author

Mark Rowh is a writer and educator based in Dublin, Virginia. His seventeen years of experience as an educator have included administrative positions at colleges in Virginia, West Virginia, and South Carolina.

Rowh is a widely published writer. His articles on education, management, and general interest topics have appeared in more than sixty national magazines. He is the author of a number of other books including *Winning Government Grants and Contracts for Your Small Business* (McGraw-Hill), *Coping with Stress in College* (College Board Books), and several entries in the VGM Career Horizons series.

Acknowledgments

The author greatly appreciates the cooperation of the following in the development of this book:

Henry Aitchison
American Association of Woodturners
American Bladesmith Society
American Craft Council
American Farriers Association
American Federation of Violin and Bow Makers
American Horticultural Therapy Association
American Institute of Organbuilders
American Watch Association
Arrowsmith School of Arts and Crafts
Artist-Blacksmith Association of North America
Association of Medical Illustrators
Blenko Glass Company
Book Manufacturers Institute
Clarissa School of Fashion Design
Doll Artisan Guild
Deb Erskine
Gemological Institute of America
Graphic Artists Guild
Great Divide Weaving School
Greeting Card Creative Network

Handweavers Guild of America
Haystack Mountain School
Horizons
International Federation of Leather Guilds
International Guild of Candle Artisans
International Guild of Taxidermy
Joseph Bulova School
Kendall College of Art and Design
Knifemakers Guild
Landing School
National Council on Education for the Ceramic Arts
North Bennet School
Peters Valley Craft Center
Pilchuck Glass School
Professional Picture Framers Association
Rhode Island School of Design
Roberto-Venn School of Luthiery
Linda Rowh
Society of American Florists
Society of North American Goldsmiths
Texarkana College
Touchstone Center for Crafts
Violin Society of America
Washington Calligraphers Guild
Watermark Association of Artisans

Foreword

The Association of Crafts & Creative Industries defines a craft as producing an item that has intrinsic value. From the single act of creation, many people have moved on to various methods to turn their ideas, visions, and creative talents into worthy careers. The Association of Crafts & Creative Industries has a membership of over 4,800 professionals including retailers, finished handcrafts manufactures, wholesalers, consultant-designer-teachers, publishers, manufacturers, and manufacturer's representatives.

Over the many years that I've been associated with this industry, I've found it remarkable to listen to the stories on how people have started with one single project, design, or activity and turned that into a successful business. In my observation, I have come to realize that our industry is what it is today because people have taken basic materials and added value through education and effort to make this the creative craft industry that it is today.

All of you who have that dream, idea, and talent please do pursue it. It is our hope that you have much success, for your success will be the success of our industry and its growth.

Walter E. Offinger
Executive Director
Association of Crafts & Creative Industries

Introduction

We live in a highly industrialized world. Mass produced goods make life easier for everyone. From automobiles to video cassette players, the products cranked out by modern factories meet our needs for food, clothing, transportation, and entertainment. There is an alternative, however, to the mass production techniques used to produce most consumer items. Have you ever admired a hand-made quilt? Drunk coffee from a hand-crafted mug? Gazed upon a beautiful blown glass vase? If so, you have appreciated the work of individual craftspersons.

Craftspersons work differently than people in other occupations. Instead of churning out thousands of products in an assembly-line process, they tend to create their works one at a time, often by hand. They carry on an old tradition from our cultural past, producing items that show the stamp of individuality.

Because their work differs so much from other occupations, many craftspersons pursue unusual careers and life-styles. The work of a blacksmith or weaver, for example, is far removed from the office, the board room, or the typical factory. And that's the thrust of this book.

Careers for Crafty People profiles a wide range of careers in various craft areas. For some people, such careers fall too far outside the "mainstream" to be considered. But for others, such career possibilities represent a godsend—a chance to do work which is creative, different, and enjoyable. This book is directed to the latter category, as well as to those who may be in a position to influence potential craftspersons. It is the author's hope that the information presented here will be not only interesting, but genuinely helpful to those making career plans which may include craft areas.

CHAPTER ONE

Jobs for Crafty People

A re you a crafty person? *Crafty* here refers not to being clever or devious, but rather a more specialized application of the term. A crafty person is one with an eye for beauty. A crafty person is someone who takes basic materials such as wood, leather, metal, or glass and painstakingly transforms them into functional or decorative products. A crafty person is one who uses patience and vision to create objects which are attractive, practical, or both. Usually, this means working with one's hands—as indicated by the "dexterous types" in this book's title. Too, crafty people take an individualized rather than an assembly-line approach to their work.

Being a crafty person can mean enjoying crafts as a hobby, or even just reading and thinking about the possibilities in this area. But it can also form the foundation of an enjoyable and productive career. In an era of computers, fax machines, and space travel, there is still a place for people with the dedication to make things by hand and in so doing to enhance the lives of others with their creativity.

A Crafty Success Story

Kathryn Lehotsky of Chillicothe, Ohio, is a crafty person. A former university administrator, she gave up her job twelve years ago to pursue her first love, Norwegian Rosemaling, on a full-time basis. This unusual craft consists of painting flower forms and scrollwork on functional items.

When she first made the move to full-time craftsperson, Lehotsky knew she would enjoy the work, but wondered if she could achieve financial success. Fortunately, the business took off, and she has done well.

"I've been able to put my son through college," she notes, "and that has been nice." She apportions her time between creating her works and selling them, largely at craft fairs. Some of her most popular works include intricately painted wooden boxes, bowls, plates, lap desks, and cupboards.

Although Lehotsky enjoys her work, she is pragmatic about her situation. "I see this as a career," she says, "not a hobby. You can't just do art for art's sake." She says craftspersons must reconcile their own artistic preferences with a sense of what people will buy. In fact, sometimes the customer's wishes take top priority.

"At first, I'd paint anything for money," she recalls. One woman had her apply flowers to a wooden toilet seat to be used as a frame for a picture of her husband. A man asked her to paint the side of a sixty-foot replica of a Viking ship (she passed on that one). She still takes on customized projects but feels free to choose her own designs and projects.

Today, she enjoys an enviable life-style. She paints in a studio in a restored century-old house overlooking the Ohio River, working about eleven months a year. She also travels frequently in several states to arts and crafts fairs, where she finds interacting with customers an interesting segment of her work.

Lehotsky urges anyone interested in a crafts career to give it a try, at least on a part-time basis. "Don't be intimidated," she says. "It's all a matter of steps. You work, you learn, and you become more professional. It can be a great life."

Your Own Success Story

Maybe *you* are a crafty person. If you're active now in one or more crafts—or if you have potential in such an area—then a crafts-related career may be a real possibility.

In considering such an option, it is important to realize that people such as Kathryn Lehotsky (and others featured in later chapters) *do* enjoy success at crafts-related careers. Certainly, such careers are a far cry from the typical office or business setting, and sometimes following a crafts career can be risky, but others have made a go of it. Maybe you can, too! After all, there are a variety of job possibilities for crafty people.

Jobs in Industry

Thousands of men and women hold jobs in industry which involve the creation of objects of beauty. The glass industry is one example. Men and women in this industry make everything from dinnerware to ornamental vases. Another example is the jewelry industry. Someone makes all those gorgeous rings that make brides gasp. These workers are definitely crafty people! Ditto for those who create all kinds of products ranging from handmade leather belts to finely crafted wood products.

Of course, some jobs in industry revolve more around the operation of machinery for mass production than the individualized work most people would consider crafts. But within the overall manufacturing establishment, plenty of opportunities can be found for the creative and dexterous person.

Jobs as Self-Employed Craftspersons

Probably the ultimate job for the crafty person is to function as a self-employed artisan. Here, the skills of a given craft form the basis for a small business. The concept is simple: you work at home (or in your own shop or studio), applying your creative talents to the production of items that appeal not only to yourself, but also to customers who will pay enough money to keep you in business.

Sound far-fetched? Or too simplistic? The truth is, over a hundred thousand people in the United States are currently self-employed as artists or craftspersons, according to the U.S. Department of Labor. This includes painters and sculptors as well as "craft-artists" and artist printmakers. It does not include many thousands more who are self-employed in related areas ranging from photography to interior design.

Certainly, making a financial success of a self-run crafts business represents a challenge. But it can be done, as ambitious people throughout the United States and Canada have proven. Jobs as self-employed craftspersons offer the promise of interesting work, creative freedom, and a chance to perform work which is far removed from that routinely done in offices and factories every day.

Jobs in Education

Most craft areas are somewhat specialized. This means that newcomers need help in learning the techniques involved, and even those with experience can often benefit from additional instruction. Accordingly, there is a great demand for people who can teach various craft areas to others.

Craft schools, community colleges, universities, art colonies, summer camps for children—these and other organizations employ people to teach in craft areas. Some schools specialize in one or two types of crafts. Others offer a wide range of subjects. The teachers they hire may be full-time educators or experienced craftspersons who teach part time as a way to sharpen their own skills and enhance their income.

In any case, teaching offers an alternative career track for those interested in crafts. For those with the right skills and knowledge—and the ability to communicate with others—teaching can help make dreams of a crafts career a reality.

Jobs Related to Crafts

Job possibilities also exist in areas that support the development and merchandising of crafts. Selling craft supplies, managing professional associations of people interested in crafts, and writing about crafts are just some options. These occupations provide alternatives for those interested in crafts, but whose interests or skills do not include the creative process of craft development itself.

Jobs in peripheral areas such as these also provide working artisans with other career possibilities if they tire of making a living exclusively as craftspersons, but would still like to be connected to the crafts world.

Advantages of a Crafts Career

A crafts career offers many advantages. First of all, it gives creative people a way to follow their true interests. One of the saddest situations in everyday life is the trapped feeling many people have about jobs they hold but do not like. Those with artistic abilities who follow crafts careers usually avoid this feeling. Instead, they work at something they actually enjoy doing!

Another advantage is that both part-time and full-time career paths can be followed. People who already have good jobs need not give them up. Homemakers, students, retired people, and others can decide just how much time they would like to devote to a craft-related endeavor, then proceed according to their own wishes. On the other hand, those who develop a broad enough base of financial support may make working as a craftsperson their full-time vocation.

The possibility of working at home is another plus. In many craft areas, most or all of the work can be performed at home.

This is a real advantage for people who find it inconvenient to commute to and from the workplace on a daily basis. For example, parents of small children who prefer to provide their own child care instead of relying on babysitters or day-care centers may find working at home advantageous. Similarly, people with physical disabilities can thrive in home-based craft businesses. For many disabled people, the home is the one place they find least challenging in terms of physical barriers.

In addition to these advantages, following are some other reasons a crafts career can be worth pursuing.

Ten Reasons to Consider a Crafts-Related Career

1. It can be fun.

2. You get to express yourself.

3. The end result is a tangible product featuring beauty, practicality, or both.

4. You don't have to dress up to do your daily work.

5. Many crafts careers provide the opportunity to operate your own business.

6. You don't need four years of college to prepare for many crafts careers.

7. The potential exists to earn a good income.

8. Selling the crafts you produce can provide a chance to socialize with customers and with other craftspersons.

9. If you are self-employed, you can set your own work schedule.

10. Making crafts can be less stressful than many other types of work, if it's something you truly enjoy.

Disadvantages of a Crafts Career

No career is absolutely perfect or devoid of risks. Like other career areas, work in a crafts field has its downside.

A factor to keep in mind is that many craft areas depend on customers who have plenty of discretionary income, thus the craftspersons are particularly vulnerable to economic troubles. In a recession, an engraver is more likely to be out of work than is a nurse.

Not only are most craft areas highly dependent on economic conditions, but they require a large enough population to support sufficient business volume. This may make life difficult for craftspersons in sparsely populated areas, even though many crafts are associated with America's rural heritage. Quite often, it means that craftspersons must be willing to travel to arts and crafts fairs, exhibitions, wholesalers, or other outlets for their work.

If your aim is to become wealthy, then this field may be a poor choice. While many artisans are able to support themselves through their work, few find that crafts lead them to affluence. But if wealth is less important to you than job satisfaction and the other advantages noted previously, the financial side may still be satisfactory.

Do You Have the Right Qualifications?

A crafts career can be rewarding, but it won't be the right choice for everyone. Before pursuing work in this area, ask yourself the following questions:

	Yes	No
1. Do you enjoy making things with your hands?		
2. Do you have a good eye for details (such as shapes and colors)?		

	Yes	No
3. Are you patient? (Can you work for a long period of time at a single task or series of tasks?)	_____	_____
4. Are you creative?	_____	_____
5. Can you work well by yourself?	_____	_____
6. Are you a task-oriented person? (Do you find satisfaction in completing one task and then going on to another?)	_____	_____
7. Are you willing to go to school or to work under the supervision of someone else to learn special techniques?	_____	_____
8. Would you be willing to work in a shop-type environment?	_____	_____
9. Do you have the physical endurance to work at a craft for sufficient hours to be productive?	_____	_____
10. Can you maintain enough interest in a craft to make it more than just a hobby?	_____	_____

A Crafty Life-Style

All things considered, one of the most attractive features of a crafts-related career is the alternative life-style it can make possible. This varies not only with the type of craft, but also with the specific job being done. Making jewelry, for instance, can be a highly standardized industrial process, where employees punch time clocks and work in an assembly-line mode. Or it can be a home-based business where the craftsperson sets her or his own working hours and exercises close control of the entire creative and production process.

It is the latter picture which fits more closely the role of the truly independent craftsperson. Doing what you want and controlling your own schedule may be just a dream for most people. But for those whose occupations consist of creating handcrafted items, a great deal of freedom *is* possible.

One craftsperson puts it this way: "It can be two o'clock on a hot Monday afternoon, and if I want to, I can be floating on an inner tube in the middle of the pond near my home. Sometimes it feels great to be doing something like that. I just close my eyes and picture all those people running around in three-piece suits and fighting the rat race."

Of course, that craftsperson may be working away late at night or on a weekend. But the trade-off is a sense of freedom and self-control that few careers can duplicate.

Career Options

Given the advantages of a crafts career, the next question might be: What types of jobs are available? The following chapters will provide an overview of some of these career possibilities. If you are a crafty person—or you know someone who is—here are some craft areas that anyone might consider who holds interest in this fascinating occupational area.

CHAPTER TWO

Into the Wood

Wood. It's among the most common of building materials, and one of the oldest. People have been working with wood since the dawn of history. For those with a crafty bent, it has provided material to be carved, cut, shaped, polished, and otherwise rendered into objects offering not just practicality, but also great beauty. Today, craftspersons create an incredible array of products from wood.

Advantages of Wood

From soft white pine to durable oak, wood provides an attractive medium for crafts-related endeavors. Here are just some of the advantages of working with this unique material.

WOOD IS PLENTIFUL. Despite the concerns of some environmentalists, there is plenty of wood in the world. North America still has more trees than it needs, and current strategies of replacing trees with new ones will assure this in the future.

WOOD IS AFFORDABLE. Sure, a trip to the local lumber store can be an eye-opener. Costs seem especially high when compared with prices of a generation ago. But when compared with other materials, wood is still a reasonably priced commodity. Craftspersons can afford to purchase wood, add the cost of their labor, and still come up with products affordable to consumers.

WOOD CAN BE BEAUTIFUL. When handled with care and skill, wood provides an extremely beautiful construction material. Who can dispute the attractiveness of an elegant cherry table or mahogany chair?

WOOD OFFERS VARIETY. Because there are so many varieties and grades of wood, those who work with it can choose from a wide range of choices in basic materials. Whatever the task at hand, some type of wood is likely to meet the need.

The types of jobs that involve woodcraft are surprisingly diverse. Following is an overview of some of the most interesting of these career options.

Furniture Maker

Making furniture is one of the most basic of craft areas. It is also one of the most promising from a business viewpoint, since the items produced are functional in nature and thus appeal to a widely diverse audience.

Walt and Vicky Whitmire of Newton, North Carolina, make furniture for a living. Their family-run business, Whitmire Woodwork, has grown to include their daughter, son-in-law, and grandson.

It wasn't always that way. Walt learned his craft by working in a furniture factory for twenty-five years before branching out on his own. The hours were long, and there was no sense of personal freedom. "Some days I didn't see the sun at all," he recalls.

But then he started making and selling his own pieces as a part-time job. The business grew, and his wife, Vicky, learned the basics of the craft and joined in. Then they took the giant step of pursuing the business full time. "We didn't have much at first," Walt recalls. "We drove around with a pickup truck and a cattle trailer, wrapping the furniture in blankets and sheets. It was really a sight!" The Whitmires sold their furniture at craft fairs, and as their reputation grew, they also did custom work on request. Their volume of business increased, and today the business provides work for several family members.

The Whitmires build tables, chairs, shelves, children's furniture—virtually anything that will sell. If scrap wood is left over from one project, they come up with a design that fits its size and shape. For example, they recently developed a design for beautiful wooden bows, modeled after ribbon bows used with gift wrap, which can be used as wall or door decorations. They get ideas for new pieces from magazines, other woodworkers, and customers. They also like to visit antique shops and then develop their own versions of classic furniture.

Today, they own two vans and a twenty-foot trailer. They also enjoy a healthy demand for the furniture they build.

"We work together and we travel together," says Walt, noting that they display their work at crafts fairs up and down the East Coast. "It's a lot better than working in a factory. It has kept our family together!"

The Whitmires are just one example of success in building a career out of making furniture. An advantage with this craft area is that special training may not be necessary, nor are unusual artistic talents required. Certainly, it helps to have a flair for working with wood, good manual skills, and an eye for symmetry. But beyond these basic traits, virtually anyone can learn the fundamentals of making some type of furniture.

When it comes to furniture making, you can go the route of simplicity or of complex design and development. For example, one approach is to concentrate on just a few basic items. The first step is obtaining a design for one type of furniture, such as a stool or a bookshelf. This might be a drawing of one's own design or a copy of an existing piece of furniture. The craftsperson then simply duplicates as many copies of the original as time allows and market conditions will support.

Typical examples of furniture items which can be made in this manner include:

- Full-sized rocking chairs
- Children's rocking chairs
- Chests
- Toy boxes
- Stools
- Bookshelves
- Porch swings
- Toolboxes

As skills develop, the experienced furniture maker may choose to vary designs and emphasize individualism rather than replication of a few basic designs. Under this approach, the development of new and different pieces is an important component of the craft. At any rate, making handcrafted furniture can provide more than enough variety to keep an ambitious craftsperson busy and challenged.

Furniture Designer

Closely connected with making furniture is designing it as an artistic venture. Here, furniture is seen not just as a utilitarian item, but rather a form of art.

In this context, furniture making takes on a more complex character. Some people who follow this approach prefer to explore the subject in special workshops, classes, or extended programs of study. Many schools and craft centers offer courses in designing and making furniture. An example is the Anderson Ranch Arts Center in Snowmass Village, Colorado, which offers

workshops on such subjects as Exploring Chairs, Willow Furniture, and Advanced Furniture Making.

It is even possible to earn a college degree in furniture design.
Kendall College of Art and Design, located in Grand Rapids,
Michigan, offers a bachelor's degree with a furniture design
major. This is anything but a trendy new program, having been
in existence since 1928, yet it is quite up-to-date, even including instruction in computer design techniques. Students in this
program learn to design wood furniture products that can be
manufactured by the furniture industry, thus their work centers
more on the design of furniture than its actual production. In
the process, though, they often build prototype models of their
creations.

Typical courses in this program include the following:

Furniture Design Portfolio Review

Furniture Studio

Ornaments

Detailing I, II, III, and IV

Furniture Design I and II

Furniture Construction

Original Design

Furniture Design Thesis

Furniture Design Portfolio

In addition to major courses, students take other courses needed
for a college degree, including a number of traditional college
courses such as English and other general studies.

A college degree in furniture design? you might ask yourself.
*Can't I just study existing furniture and then come up with my
own variations?* The answer is, of course you can! The Kendall
College plan just represents one option. Or you can enroll in a
short course such as those offered by the Anderson Ranch Arts

Center. Another approach is to learn as much as you can about furniture—read books on the subject, prowl around furniture stores and antique shops—and then try your hand at a few simple designs.

Once you master the basics of designing furniture, you may want to operate solely in this area. Or like many craftspersons, you can combine the skills of furniture design with the actual practice of furniture making.

For more information:

Kendall College of Art and Design
   11 Division Avenue North
   Grand Rapids, MI 49503-3194

Anderson Ranch Arts Center
   P.O. Box 5598
   Snowmass Village, CO 81615

Woodturner

In a less functional direction, woodturners produce beautiful work which may be purely decorative. Woodturners produce this fascinating work using lathes or other equipment to cut, shape, and polish wood. The result ranges from sculptures to unusual wood containers.

Just some examples of this work:

- A New York woodturner produces segmented turnings that resemble woven and stitched baskets.
- A Wasington-based craftsperson makes turnings that emulate desert scenes and other landscapes.
- A Vermont woodturner makes attractive lidded containers.

Other woodturners produce large and small sculptures, holiday ornaments, goblets, various kinds of vessels, and other items.

While some men and women practice wood turning as a hobby, others pursue it as a part-time or full-time career. Many specialize in just a few types of products, while others take a more broad-based approach. They sell their work through galleries, crafts fairs, trade shows, and direct marketing.

James Edward Barnes works as a woodturner out of his home in Ridgeway, Virginia. Formerly employed as an industrial designer, he used his design skills in mastering the craft of turning wood. Then when he was laid off from his full-time job three years ago, he turned to wood turning as an alternative occupation.

"It's a much less stressful job," he says. "I used to take a lot of antacid, but not anymore." He grants that his income level is lower, but he says he enjoys the freedom involved. "I get to do what I want to do, when I want to do it."

Barnes owns five lathes which he uses to produce beautiful bowls and vessels. He sells most of his work through galleries. He has tried craft shows but believes his works may be too expensive for the average browser at such events.

The first step at becoming a woodturner, he says, is learning to use a lathe. Then it takes patience and practice to learn the craft. He notes that in his experience, most woodturners combine their work with teaching or other jobs, or pursue their craft along with retirement. According to Barnes, newcomers can obtain a lathe and basic cutting tools for about $500. Experienced woodturners, he adds, may invest up to $25,000 in their equipment.

One way to get started in wood turning is to enroll in a course or seminar on the subject. Another way is to contact someone who works in this area and work out an apprenticeship or other plan for working with, and learning from, an experienced woodturner.

Anyone who is serious about wood turning as a career should take advantage of membership in the American Association of Woodturners (AAW). This group has over forty local chapters across the United States and is also open to members from Canada and other countries.

The AAW publishes a quarterly journal, *American Woodturner*. A staple of this magazine is how-to information on various aspects of woodturning. It also includes valuable information on topics ranging from book reviews to safety tips.

An annual highlight is a three-day symposium held in a different part of the country each year. The event includes demonstrations by recognized woodturners, an "instant gallery" where members can display their work, and a trade show.

Of special note is the group's scholarship program, which provides funds to attend classes in wood turning offered by a number of craft schools. Only AAW members are eligible to receive scholarship funds.

For more information:

American Association of Woodturners
667 Harriet Avenue
Shoreview, MN 55126

Woodcarver

Woodcarvers play a unique role in the world of arts and crafts. They produce decorative and artistic items, as well as making functional items more attractive.

Some craftspersons use power equipment—sometimes even a chain saw—to produce carvings. Others work entirely by hand, using chisels, knives, or other hand cutting tools.

To make a go of working full-time at their craft, many woodcarvers specialize in a single type of product or a series of related items. Here are just some examples:

- Carving fish, ducks, or other animals to cater to the interests of hunters and others with a love of the outdoors
- Producing items related to local or regional culture (such as figures of "mountaineers" and other Appalachian characters in the southeastern United States)
- Carving canes or walking sticks for use in hiking, or related items
- Creating wooden busts or statues.

In some instances, craftspersons in this field apply their skills to materials other than wood. For instance, animal bones may be used as an alternative to wood. The same is true of the antlers of deer or elk. And some enterprising carvers have learned to use a nut-based substitute for ivory as a raw material that meets today's standards for protecting the environment.

Toy Maker

In the age of Nintendo, is there still a place for wooden toys? Perhaps surprisingly, the answer is a definite yes. Not only do today's computer-literate children still enjoy playing with wooden toys, but many adults will go out of their way to purchase "old-fashioned" toys for their children and grandchildren. There is something inherently satisfying about a genuine wood toy, especially one that has been handcrafted.

Craftspersons who make toys produce a wide variety of items, including dinosaurs, trains, carousel animals, and guns.

Wooden toys are often popular items at craft shows. They are also sold to specialty shops and other retailers (for instance, toy wooden cannons might be sold to a store that features Civil War merchandise). For those who enjoy making them, wooden toys can be an adjunct to other types of woodworking, or an area of special focus.

Guitar Maker

To be a successful craftsperson from a career viewpoint, one must create products that are in significant demand by the public at large, or that meet the needs of a specific interest group. People who make guitars fall into the latter category. After all, guitars are among the most popular of instruments. The glamour of rock and roll, the popularity of country music, and the appeal of other types of music involving guitars make these instruments in great demand. This is true not only for professional musicians who often treasure handcrafted instruments, but also for countless music lovers who simply enjoy playing guitars.

People who make guitars may operate their own businesses or work for companies that manufacture and sell musical instruments. Some build only acoustic guitars; others specialize in electric guitars; still others make both kinds of instruments. Although other materials may be used, wood is still a basic building material. Favorite woods for this purpose include mahogany, spruce, cedar, and rosewood, with different types of wood used for different parts of the instrument.

The Roberto-Venn School of Luthiery in Phoenix, Arizona, provides a comprehensive program in guitar making. The basic course consists of 720 hours of instruction offered over a four-month period. During this time, every student constructs at least one acoustic and one electric guitar. For more information, contact the school:

Roberto-Venn School of Luthiery
4011 South 16th Street
Phoenix, AZ 85040

Violin Maker

Among the most specialized of all woodcrafts is the work of those who make violins. Their work rests on centuries of tradition, including master craftspersons such as Antonio Stradivari, whose seventeenth-century violins are considered perhaps the finest ever made.

Since violins play a central role in orchestras and other highly formal musical settings, they must be made to exacting standards. Violin makers work slowly and carefully, and their work may be subject to review by others in the field.

Unlike some craft areas, violin making is not something that can be readily self-taught. Perhaps the best way to get started is to contact a practicing violin maker and discuss possibilities for learning the craft. The American Federation of Violin and Bow Makers publishes a directory of its members in the United States, Canada, and France. To obtain a copy, write to the address at the end of this section. Or check the yellow pages in your phone book to see if a craftsperson is listed. The Violin Society of America, whose members include both those who make these instruments and violin players, is another source of information.

For more information:

American Federation of Violin and Bow Makers
33 N. "B" Street
San Mateo, CA 94401

Violin Society of America
614 Lerew Road
Boiling Springs, PA 17001-9500

Traditional Instrument Maker

In the Old World and later in colonial America, a variety of handmade instruments served roles similar to those of guitars, violins, and other related instruments. These included banjos, mandolins, dulcimers, and other related instruments, some of which are still made today.

Ken Hamblin of Salem, Virginia, makes dulcimers, banjos, and autoharps, which he sells at craft shows and by mail. His specialty is the Appalachian dulcimer, a three- or four-string instrument made in either a teardrop or hourglass shape. Built of walnut or cherry, the beautiful instruments are popular with traditional musicians as well as those interested in music and culture of the past.

In addition to the Appalachian dulcimer, Hamblin makes hammered dulcimers. These larger instruments, constructed of maple and red cedar, are played with a small hammer not unlike that used for a xylophone. Hamblin also makes maple autoharps and other items.

The craftsperson who chooses to make traditional instruments can gain satisfaction not only from the work itself, but also in the knowledge that the culture of the past is being preserved. To learn more about this unique craft area, visit a crafts fair or a performance by musicians using traditional instruments, and talk with those involved. Some summer arts and crafts programs also offer classes or seminars on making traditional instruments.

Cabinetmaker

A major occupation in the woodworking field is that of cabinetmaking. Obviously, this specialty is closely related to making furniture of other types. The differences in the two vocations fall largely in the scope of work that may be undertaken. Unlike those who produce a variety of furniture types, cabinetmakers tend to focus on a few basic items: cabinets, shelves, counters, and related structures used in homes and businesses for storage or work space.

Another distinguishing feature of this field is that work may be done not only in a shop or factory, but also on site in homes or businesses. In one instance, a cabinetmaker may build kitchen cabinets in a shop and then install them in a customer's home. In another case, the cabinetmaker might do the basic construction where it is to be located, installing a set of built-in shelves which are not designed to be portable.

In the spectrum of careers that involve working with wood, cabinetmaking would probably fall somewhere in the middle. The work generally is not as artistic as that of a woodcarver, nor is it as elemental and varied as that of a carpenter, who may build anything from crude wooden forms for pouring concrete to the rough structures of inner walls and subfloors.

Cabinetmakers' work is careful, methodical, and precise. Their work is production-oriented, but it also has its creative side. Choosing a cabinet design or creating a new one can be a challenging process. Similarly, putting just the right finish on a shelf or cabinet is not that different from the work of the artist.

Cabinetmakers use tools and techniques not greatly different from those of others who work with wood. They learn their craft in any of several ways, from classes or seminars to on-the-job training. Perhaps the best way to get started in this field is to hire out to an experienced cabinetmaker and learn the craft as a part-time or full-time employee. Studying books and magazine articles on the subject can also help (see list at end of this chapter).

Boat Builder

Another specialized job category is that of boat builder. People who construct wooden boats fill a unique niche. They build various types of boats, with sailboats as perhaps the most glamorous.

Workers in this field may specialize in constructing small boats, building cruising boats, or designing various types of craft. Some are employed by companies that build boats and ships, by design firms, or by marine supply companies. Others operate their own businesses building or repairing boats.

A school that specializes in this field offers students complete ten-month programs in either boat building or design. For more information:

Landing School
P.O. Box 1490
Kennebunkport, ME 04046

Other Woodcraft Jobs

The previous sections described just some of the careers that involved the craft of working with wood. Here are a few more brief examples.

MODEL MAKER Some people specialize in building wooden models of boats, buildings, or other structures. For example, one artisan builds small wooden replicas of airplanes. Pilots and other flight lovers buy the small pieces not as toys, but as decorations or mementos.

BIRDHOUSE MAKER Birdhouses are popular items everywhere. Some craftspersons build birdhouses and feeders and then sell them in various versions: painted, unpainted, fully assembled, or partially assembled.

MANTEL MAKER In older homes, mantels above fireplaces were a staple. A South Carolina craftsperson has found there is a growing demand for mantels in newer homes as well. He operates a full-time business designing, building, and installing mantels of various sizes and configurations.

CARPENTER Carpenters represent a more mainstream craft than many others discussed in this chapter, but they apply similar skills, use the same kinds of tools, and offer the chance for interesting, gratifying work. From building a storage shed or constructing temporary scaffolding to installing finely crafted molding in a home or office, carpenters perform a wide range of tasks.

A more specialized version of the carpenter's role is that of the preservation carpenter. Workers in this field help restore and preserve historic buildings and other items constructed in earlier times.

WOODBURNER Instead of carving, practitioners of this craft burn images into wood. The letters and graphic designs which result combine both practical and decorative features. For example, some works serve as simple signs, while others represent artistic creations.

FURNITURE RESTORER This field involves refinishing and otherwise restoring older furniture. Some people who work in this field handle only the finishes of furniture, while others acquire skills similar to those used in making furniture and reconstruct portions of damaged pieces.

Further Reading

Books

American Woodworker Woodworking Techniques. Rodale Press, 1988.

The Art of Woodturning. American Craft, 1983.

Banister, Manly. *Making Picture Frames in Wood*. Sterling Publishing, 1981.

Bigelow, B. William. *Woodworking Techniques, Tips and Projects from a Master Craftsman*. Tab Books, 1989.

Calhoun, Ben. *Complete Guide to Professional Woodworking*. Prentice-Hall, 1989.

Feirer, John. *Furniture and Cabinet Making: A Complete How-to by America's Foremost Expert on Woodworking*. Macmillan, 1983.

Joyce, Ernest. *Encyclopedia of Furniture Making*. Sterling Publishing, 1989.

Mader, Josef. *Chip Carving & Relief Carving*. Macmillan, 1987.

Spence, William, and L. Duane Griffiths. *The Woodworker's Illustrated Benchtop Reference*. Tab Books, 1989.

Underhill, Roy. *The Woodwright's Companion: Exploring Traditional Woodcraft*. University of North Carolina Press, 1983.

Wheeler, William, and Charles Hayward. *Woodcarving*. Sterling Publishing, 1972.

In addition to these books, those interested in woodworking may want to check out the Woodworkers Book Club, P.O. Box 12171, Cincinnati, OH 45212-0171.

Magazines

American Woodworking
    35 E. Minor Street
    Emmaus, PA 18098

Art Business News
    Box 3837
    Stamford, CT 06905

Fine Woodworking
    P.O. Box 5506
    Newton, CT 06470

Popular Woodworking
    1320 Galaxy Way
    Concord, CA 94520

Woodshop News
    35 Pratt Street
    Essex, CT 06426-1185

Woodwork
    Ross Periodicals
    P.O. Box 1529
    Ross, CA 94957

CHAPTER THREE

All That Glitters

The human eye has always been attracted to beauty—especially the kind that shines or glitters. From the tombs of the pharaohs to the palaces of eighteenth-century Europe and on to the present, people from all types of cultures and all walks of life have placed special value on items that catch light and reflect or refract it. If the materials from which such objects were made held great value, such as precious jewels or metals, so much the better.

People who can work with jewels or various kinds of metal have long been in demand. Today, craftspersons in a wide range of specialty areas meet the needs for finely crafted objects made of these materials.

Jewelry Maker

Want to work at a craft that is not only creative, but also a great source of potential profits? If so, consider the role of jewelry maker. This craft combines the pleasure of creating beautiful work with the practicality of a product for which people will pay a premium. While some crafts appeal only to customers with specialized interests (for example, making dulcimers or mandolins), jewelry holds value to almost anyone. Even those who are not in the market for jewelry for themselves may be potential buyers of gift items for relatives and friends.

Jewelry makers may be known by any of several titles including jeweler, jewelry jobber, and jewelry repairer. They design, construct, and repair all types of jewelry including rings, necklaces, bracelets, pins, and earrings. Their work is not only artistic, but also very detailed and quite precise.

Janette and Walter Jager of Franklin, North Carolina, work together in a full-time jewelry making business. Like many crafts professionals, they first held other jobs while pursuing their craft on a part-time basis. She was a nurse, and he was a pianist. But then they took the jump to a full-time craft business and are glad they did.

"It's great being your own boss," Janette says. "You don't have to punch a clock. Actually, we probably work more hours now than before. But we can use our creativity, and are free to do anything we want."

The Jagers make rings, wire bracelets, and other items. They work primarily with 14-karat gold and sterling silver. Their work involves not just making jewelry, but displaying and selling it. Attending thirty to forty craft shows a year from Florida to Pennsylvania, they work as a team. While one staffs their booth, the other works on making new jewelry in an open format which attracts the interest of customers.

"An advantage to this kind of business is that we can work together," Janette notes. "It's a lot of hard work, but a lot of fun, too."

The Jagers advise others to proceed carefully before making the commitment to a full-time business. "Find out what kind of talent you have first," Janette says. "Then see if you can build up some business part-time. If you can, take classes from a craft school or someone else who knows the business."

Some workers who make jewelry operate in a manufacturing setting. A typical job might involve placing gems in rings as part of a team assembling jewelry in a factory. Another job might consist of cleaning and repairing jewelry as a staff member in a jewelry store. Other jobs, like the Jagers', involve designing and making pieces as a small business.

Jewelers usually develop their skills through on-the-job training or by attending a trade or technical school. Those who attend trade schools take classes in such subjects as basic jewelry making skills, repair techniques, and use of tools and machines. Programs normally take two years or less to complete.

Gem Cutter

A less common occupation than jewelry maker—but a very important related one—is that of gem cutter. Gem cutters take rough gemstones and cut, grind, or polish them into the gleaming gems needed to make beautiful rings, necklaces, bracelets, and other types of jewelry.

Some gem cutters work for jewelry companies. Others operate their own businesses. In the latter case, they either work on a contractual basis for wholesale or retail firms, or they directly purchase uncut gems and then sell them after rendering them usable for jewelry.

Even more than in most craft areas, working as a gem cutter requires patience. In fact, it takes a very special type of personality to be able to succeed in, and to enjoy, this unique field. Successful gem cutters are able to sit quietly in one position for long periods of time. They have (or are able to develop) a knack for pacing themselves, working quickly enough to be productive, yet slowly and carefully enough to avoid costly mistakes. The latter is a key consideration. Mistakes in gem cutting can be disastrous, given the value that precious gems usually carry.

Not only is the work precise and painstaking, but it also involves a certain sense of vision. A gem cutter must be able to take a rough hunk of material and in his or her mind's eye see it as a lovely, shining gem. Then, the cutter must employ the necessary techniques to bring about such a transformation. This usually involves cutting or grinding the gem in such a way that any extraneous material is removed, and shaping (such as facets) is added to reflect light and enhance the stone's beauty. The mental effort involved might be compared to that of a champion chess player, who must envision moves far in advance of making them. In shaping the material at hand, the gem cutter must think ahead, anticipate problems, and make the most of each cut or change.

In addition to the demands of the work itself, gem cutting is a challenging vocation. This is especially true of the independent gem cutter. Such a role may require a substantial financial investment. Special tools, such as diamond saws, are necessary. In addition, the expense of purchasing gems such as rubies, sapphires, and emeralds—even in a rough state—can be significant.

To learn about gem cutting, a good starting point is to take a class on the subject. Classes in gem cutting are sometimes offered by community colleges or other schools. Even classes designed more for hobbyists than for professionals can prove helpful. Whatever the starting point, many elements of the craft can only be learned by actual practice in cutting gems. Working first with semiprecious stones or others of modest value is wise. Also, offering to work with an experienced gem cutter as an assistant or informal apprentice is another way to get started.

The Gemological Institute of America is a major school offering training in this area. Campuses are located in several cities around the world. For information on American campuses, write to the following addresses:

Gemological Institute of America
1660 Stewart Street
Santa Monica, CA 90404

Gemological Institute of America
580 Fifth Avenue
New York, NY 10036

Watchmaker

How about a career in horology? Horology—the art of making watches, or more generally the study of time—is an occupation that has flourished for several hundred years. Watchmakers have long enjoyed working at a craft which is highly specialized, always in demand, and financially rewarding.

The term *watchmaker* is generally used to refer not just to constructing watches, but also repairing them. In fact, much of the need for workers in this field comes in the latter category.

Few people would challenge the idea that watchmaking is indeed a craft. Those who master this complex process do detailed, precise work which can include the creative process of watch or clock design as well as the more mechanical functions of watch maintenance and repair. The products with which watchmakers deal, like those addressed by jewelry makers, are often regarded as much for their beauty as their functionality. Working with an expensive luxury watch, for instance, can be compared with building or repairing an intricate bracelet, ring, or necklace.

Despite some changes in watch technology, prospects for a career in watchmaking remain strong. There was a time a few years ago when some people were predicting the demise of traditional watchmaking and repair due to the advent of digital watches and other electronic models. But the field has survived such changes and made something of a comeback. Mechanical watches remain a popular item, especially expensive "brand name" varieties. As a result, consumers still have significant needs for the services of skilled watchmakers and repairers. In fact, the need for new workers in this field is expected to be quite strong in the next ten to fifteen years, as more and more working watchmakers reach retirement age.

To practice their craft, watchmakers and repairers must learn how different types of watches operate, and then master the use of appropriate tools. These include special lathes, grinding wheels, and electronic testing and regulating equipment. Watchmakers also use various types of measurement equipment such as metric scales, balances and micrometers, optical equipment such as microscopes, and ultrasound cleaning equipment. Their work is done at a workbench, and the surrounding environment is usually clean and relatively quiet as opposed to that of the machine shop or factory floor.

As with other craft areas, watchmakers enjoy the option of working for themselves or of seeking jobs in industry or the retail business. Typical employers include watch factories, jewelry stores, department stores, and shops specializing in the repair of jewelry and watches.

For those who prefer to operate their own business, watchmaking offers unusual opportunities. Since there is not a surplus of trained watchmakers and repairers (but rather a shortage in many parts of the country), small businesses in this field may encounter fewer problems in generating business than in many other craft areas which may be considered less essential to the ordinary customer.

In starting their own businesses, some watchmakers rent bench space while others set up operations in a garage or portion of their home. Some develop contracts with watch manufacturers or retail establishments that sell large numbers of watches. Others prefer to deal directly with individual customers.

The precise nature of watchmaking requires special training. This is available through a number of community colleges, technical colleges, and trade schools.

Probably the best known school in this field is the Joseph Bulova School located in Woodside, New York. Here, students may choose from among a nine-month program in watch repair technology, a thirteen-month program in watch repair, and a seventeen-month program in watchmaking. Typical courses include the following:

Balance Wheel Truing

Pivot Polishing and Poising

Blueprint Reading

Basic Lathe

Hairspring Manipulation

Hairspring Collating and Truing

Hairspring Vibrating

Hairspring Studding, Centering, and Overcoiling

Jewelry Repair

Assembly and Jeweling

Special Toolmaking

Basic Stems

Applied Stems

Applied Staffs

General Repair

Electronic Horology

Clock Repair

For information about this school, write to:

The Joseph Bulova School
40-24 62nd Street
Woodside, NY 11377

Because of the shortage of watchmakers in some areas, it may be possible to obtain financial sponsorship from an employer or prospective employer. In such cases, the employer may pay all or part of the student's tuition or other educational costs.

A nice feature about watchmaking is that the skills are readily transferable to other occupations. Thus, pursuing a career in watchmaking, especially trying to make a success of a one-person business, is not as risky as some other craft areas. Experienced watchmakers and repairers can readily find jobs in other areas requiring a high skill level, such as instrumentation or electronics.

For more information:

American Watch Association
1201 Pennsylvania Avenue, NW
P.O. Box 464
Washington, DC 20004

American Watchmakers Institute
3700 Harrison Avenue
Cincinnati, OH 45211

Blacksmith

Blacksmiths, once the providers to every village or town, still flourish if in much smaller numbers than in our agrarian past. Many run their own one-person shop. As in past times, working with horseshoes is a major source of business. Blacksmiths who shoe horses are also known as farriers.

Blacksmiths also construct collars, farm utensils, tools, and other practical items. Some make objects that are designed more for artistic purposes. Others specialize in a specific line of items such as skillets or other kitchen utensils.

The skills needed by a blacksmith can be mastered on an individual basis while working for or studying under an experienced blacksmith. Another approach is to take classes or summer workshops. One place to learn such techniques is the Touchstone Center for Crafts in Uniontown, Pennsylvania, where students enroll in workshops covering such topics as these:

Beginning Blacksmithing

Traditional Architectural Blacksmithing

Advanced Metals

Kitchen Smithing

For more information on the school, write:

Touchstone Center for Crafts
P.O. Box 2141
Uniontown, PA 15401

The American Farriers Association publishes a brochure listing schools throughout the United States and Canada which offer courses in this field. Just some of them include the following:

Lookout Mountain School of Horseshoeing
Gadsden, AL 35901

Tucson School of Horseshoeing
2230 North Kimberlee Road
Tucson, AZ 85749

Colorado School of Trades
1575 Hoyt Street
Lakewood, CO 80215

Far Hills Forge
P.O. Box 703
Far Hills, NJ 07931

For a complete listing, write to:

American Farriers Association
4059 Iron Works Pike
Lexington, KY 40511

Another organization of interest is the Artist-Blacksmith Association of North America (ABANA). This group serves those interested in blacksmithing as an art form. The group sponsors conferences, exhibitions, publications, and other activities. It also maintains a library of slides and videotapes showing works of blacksmiths from around the world. For information, write to:

ABANA
P.O. Box 1181
Nashville, IN 47448

Goldsmith and Silversmith

Goldsmiths work with gold and other precious metals. They make a variety of ornamental items: jewelry, desk accessories, medallions, chains, and many other items. While some goldsmiths work independently, many others work for jewelry firms or other companies.

Silversmiths do very similar work, but use silver as their primary working material. They often produce tableware and related items in addition to jewelry and other ornamental work.

Persons interested in this craft area should consider joining the Society of North American Goldsmiths (SNAG), headquartered in Tampa, Florida. While the title of the organization refers only to gold, its members work in a variety of materials including silver, copper, brass, nickel, and other metals, as well as non-metallic substances such as polymer clays, marble, quartz, pearl, and coral.

Like organizations in other craft areas, SNAG provides members a forum for networking with others who share the same interests. Members can take advantage of an annual conference, exhibitions of fine metalwork, and publications of interest. These include *Metalsmith,* a quarterly magazine, as well as a bimonthly newsletter which includes details on exhibitions, conferences, and workshops. It also lists job opportunities in the field, an extremely helpful feature for anyone interested in pursuing employment as a goldsmith or silversmith.

For more information:

Society of North American Goldsmiths
5009 Londonderry Drive
Tampa, FL 33647

Knifemaker

Knifemakers or bladesmiths use various techniques to construct knives. The most accomplished use forging methods to take steel, nickel, or other metals and create knife blades. Bladesmiths also use techniques such as grinding, filing, and annealing. They also make handles of different materials including wood, plastic, or such traditional materials as bone.

Traditional bladesmiths do most of their work by hand and may operate their own shops and businesses. An example is E. Jay Hendrickson of Frederick, Maryland. He is a master bladesmith who is also taking a turn as president of the American Bladesmith Society.

"Knifemaking as a full-time job is very possible," he notes. "It just depends on how hard one wants to work."

Hendrickson recommends starting on a small scale at first. "Treat knifemaking as a hobby until you really understand the entire process," he says. "Experience in business is a must. Make a couple hundred knives and you will understand if you want to become a knifemaker."

Those who are seriously interested in a knifemaking career might consider attending the School of Bladesmithing offered through Texarkana College of Texarkana, Texas. This unique school offers intensive classes lasting one or two weeks each, making it possible for people from around the country to attend. Courses are taught by recognized bladesmiths from Texas, Arkansas, and across the United States who teach through special arrangement with the school. Class sessions are held in Washington, Arkansas, in a replica of a one-room schoolhouse and adjacent barn. The facility includes a modern classroom as well as equipment such as forges, grinders, workbenches, and a trip-hammer. Students and faculty stay in a local hotel which offers special rates to those connected with the school. Students may enroll in courses such as the following:

INTRODUCTION TO BLADESMITHING Taught over a two-week period, this course covers the hand forging of blades. Through both lecture and hands-on work, students learn to select metal and make blades through hammer forging, annealing, heat treating, grinding, and tempering.

HANDLES AND GUARDS Students in this course take finished blades and attach handles to come up with finished knives.

DAMASCUS STEEL This course prepares participants to produce high-quality Damascus blades.

FOLDING BLADES This one-week course covers the basics of folding knife construction. Students learn to make both locking and nonlocking blades.

BLADESMITHING LAB Students take on special projects while working with instructors and one another.

Since courses are offered on a noncredit basis, students need not worry about grades. Those who complete courses receive certificates which indicate they have earned continuing education units.

It is possible to learn this craft without attending formal classes. Some people learn bladesmithing as employees or apprentices of experienced knifemakers.

A good source of information about this craft is the American Bladesmith Society. Membership in this group is open to anyone interested in bladesmithing, including working knifemakers, collectors, and others. The society publishes a quarterly newsletter and sponsors a certification program which can lead to the designation of Master Smith for those who proceed to the highest levels of this intriguing craft.

Bladesmiths sell their products to knife collectors, hunters, and others who appreciate knives of high quality. Workers in plants that manufacture knives and related products tend to use less-specialized skills, instead relying on a more mechanized process.

For more information:

Knifemakers Guild
    P.O. Box 928
    Madisonville, TN 37354

American Bladesmith Society
    4204 Ballenger Creek Pike
    Frederick, MD 21701

School of Bladesmithing
    Texarkana College
    Evening and Continuing Education Division
    2500 North Robison Road
    Texarkana, TX 75599

Related Careers

In addition to the careers previously discussed in this chapter, a variety of other occupations involve similar skills. Some, while they involve working with one's hands to create or repair different types of shiny products, might be considered more within the realm of manufacturing or production than the artsy side of crafts. At any rate, these and many other career possibilities hold promise for dexterous types everywhere.

MACHINISTS produce precision parts of metal or plastic. They build new items from printed designs or their own plans, duplicate existing objects, or make precision repairs.

IRONWORKERS build steel or iron frameworks for buildings or other structures. Some specialize in ornamental work such as producing wrought-iron building parts or furniture.

WELDERS use heat or other special processes to join metals together. Some work in heavy industries such as shipbuilding or building construction. Others use welding processes to make sculpture or pursue other more artistic endeavors.

SHEET-METAL WORKERS install, produce, or repair sheet-metal products ranging from storage buildings to outdoor signs. Some work for large construction companies. Others run their own businesses in installing aluminum siding or providing other services.

TOOL AND DIE MAKERS perform work much like that of machinists, but at a more advanced level. They produce machine parts and other metal items with an extremely high level of precision.

SOLDERERS use techniques similar to welders, working with small items such as the internal components of electronic equipment. Their work requires the same kind of patience and attention to detail as many other crafts.

PEWTERSMITHS work like silversmiths or goldsmiths. But instead of using these precious metals, they use pewter, an alloy of tin and copper.

CHAIN MAKERS build everything from fine chains used for ornamental purposes to heavier chains designed for industrial uses.

Some operate special machines for making chains, while others work by hand.

ENGRAVERS add lettering to jewelry, plaques, and other items. Once a process done exclusively by hand, engraving now may also be done through computerized methods. In either case, a continuing demand exists for skilled engravers.

TROPHY ASSEMBLERS put together trophies and plaques. Often, they work with products which have been previously manufactured, providing the finishing touches of assembly and sometimes engraving. While some trophy assemblers work as employees in factories or businesses selling trophies, others operate their own small businesses. In fact, trophy assembly can be an attractive home-based business.

Further Reading

Once you become interested in a specific craft area related to jewelry, precious metals, or other materials, it will be helpful to read specialized information on the subject. The following books may be of interest.

Bovin, Murray. *Jewelry Making for Schools, Tradesmen, Craftsmen.* Bovin, 1979.
Duke, Henry C. *Art of Gem Cutting,* 7th ed. Gem Books.
Hrisoulas, Jim. *The Master Bladesmith.* Paladin Press, 1991.
Scarsbrick, Diana. *Jewelry Design Sourcebook.* Van Nostrand Reinhold, 1989.
Von Neumann, Robert. *The Design and Creation of Jewelry.* Chilton, 1982.

CHAPTER FOUR

Glass, Clay, and Things on Display

The careers touched on in previous chapters have dealt mostly with wood and metal. But those two materials represent just a fraction of the media with which craftspersons can work. Glass, clay, wax, and flowers, among others, also provide creative people with challenging working material. This chapter takes a look at several fascinating career possibilities based on working with these and related materials.

Stained Glass Maker

Have you ever caught your breath in awe at the beauty of an intricate stained glass window as it catches the morning sunlight? If so, you're among the many admirers of stained glass.

The skill of making stained glass has become something of a rarity, but there is still a demand for this beautiful product. In fact, those who learn to make it can often find a ready market for their work.

Stained glass is usually associated with churches, and rightly so. The huge cathedrals of the Middle Ages gave artisans the chance to develop their craft to perfection. They set a standard which has held up for centuries.

While the use of stained glass may never again reach the pinnacle years of the Middle Ages, it has nevertheless survived to the present day. In fact, stained glass has enjoyed something of a resurgence in recent years. Modern-day churches still provide a demand for stained glass windows as new sanctuaries are built or existing structures expanded. Those who work in this area also find a demand for other products such as lamps, wall decorations, holiday ornaments, and suncatchers, which are small panels designed for placement on ordinary windows.

Adrienne Kinder, a stained glass specialist in Ocala, Florida, creates a variety of products including windows, lamps, and door panels. She started working part time while holding a full-time job in another field, but she now is able to sustain a full-time craft business.

"It's nearly impossible to earn a living from stained glass in the beginning," she says. "It takes patience. But with time, business grows."

Kinder is enthusiastic about the work. "I love it," she says. She recalls the satisfaction of finishing a major project such as a church window. "There's no feeling like it," she notes. "To have created something like that is very satisfying."

Kinder and other professionals recommend that newcomers to this field take one or two primary approaches to learning the craft. One is to locate an experienced craftsperson and offer to serve as an apprentice. The other is to enroll in classes taught at craft schools, summer workshops, or other educational programs.

For instance, Horizons, a New England craft school, offers intensive workshops in a variety of subjects including stained glass. A typical course, offered over a four-day period, covers pattern development, glass cutting techniques, assembly, foiling, soldering, and patina application. On a more long-term basis, the Rhode Island School of Design offers a four-year program in working with glass which includes a course in stained glass.

For more information:

Horizons
374 Old Montague Road
Amherst, MA 01002

Rhode Island School of Design
Two College Street
Providence, RI 02903-2791

Glassblower

Glassblowers produce some of the most beautiful items known to humankind. After all, glass itself, with its ability to diffract and reflect light, is inherently pretty. But when this already attractive material takes on the delicate shapes and symmetry made possible by glassblowing techniques, the results can be breathtaking. Vases, tumblers, sculptures, Christmas tree ornaments, and many other decorative and functional items are produced by glassblowers.

Blowing glass is a highly specialized craft. Those who master it hold creative, demanding jobs. Some work in factories that produce specialty glassware. Others operate as one-person businesses. Some teach their skills in schools or workshop settings.

The traditional method of blowing glass is to create molten glass and then dip a long blowpipe, made of iron, into the molten mixture. Retrieving a glob of hot glass, the craftsperson blows into the tube while rotating it. The result is a hollow glass object which has been shaped according to the desires of the glassblower.

Today, even though mass production and other facets of modern technology have made glass production a large-scale endeavor, there is still a place for manual glassblowing. Modern consumers seem to love to purchase handblown glass. In fact, people will often pay a premium for such items.

A visit to the Blenko glass factory near Milton, West Virginia, provides a fascinating look at the craft of glassblowing. Here, visitors may watch working artisans as they produce blown glass products. The slow, careful process of creating a vase, for instance, provides visitors with an inside look at the painstaking work involved. The factory also includes an outlet shop where finished pieces are sold.

Several special qualities are needed to pursue this highly specialized craft area. Chief among them are patience, an eye for proportion, stamina, and creativity. A tolerance for heat is also required. Most craftspersons in this field also hold an intense desire for perfection.

Because of its specialized nature, glassblowing is not taught as widely as are some other crafts. Some craft schools and summer programs include courses in glassblowing. An unusually diverse selection of courses is available at Pilchuck Glass School in Seattle, Washington. Courses vary from session to session, with typical examples including:

Beginning Glassblowing

Hot Glass: Historical Preferences, Modern Techniques

Master Glassblowing

Glassblowing: Sculpture from Natural Sources

For more information:

Pilchuck Glass School
107 South Main Street, No. 324
Seattle, WA 98104-2580

Potter or Ceramic Artist

Long before glass was invented, people made clay pottery. Ancient civilizations learned to shape jars, pots, vases, and even writing tablets out of clay. Though these uses were largely re-placed over time by other materials, there has always been a place for the work of potters and others who can shape clay into functional or artistic forms.

Today, potters and ceramic artists produce a variety of products ranging from simple vases to delicate figurines. Some work primarily with earthenware or stoneware, both of which are relatively heavy materials. Others specialize in working with porcelain, which is more delicate. Their methods of making pottery include using slabs or coils of clay, molds, or a potter's wheel. The craft includes not just shaping the object to be made, but also techniques such as glazing and firing.

Carol Rosenberg of Roanoke, Virginia, makes handcrafted stoneware pottery. She has been working with pottery for about fifteen years as an adjunct to her main role as a homemaker.

"I enjoy the work," she notes, but says this would be a difficult area to pursue as a full-time job. She contends that it is better suited for retired people or those who prefer part-time work. She also notes that an investment is required for basic working materials. She has spent about $2,000 for a wheel, kiln, and related materials.

"The real value is not making money," she adds, "but the satisfaction of the work itself. You can't measure that. And it's nice to bring enjoyment to others. The other day a lady just beamed when she saw a piece I had made for her. It made my whole day."

Of course, some craftspersons do make this a full-time career. Some make a go of it by specializing in more expensive items or by mass-producing a basic, popular line of products such as mugs or cups. Others combine their work with teaching. Some potters work in industry instead of operating their own businesses, work-ing for firms that produce dishware or other pottery or porcelain products.

Techniques for working with clay are widely taught. Commu-nity colleges, and the continuing education divisions of four-year colleges and universities, often offer courses and seminars to anyone who is interested. Most of these offerings are taught on a noncredit basis.

Craft schools, many of which operate only in the summer, also offer classes in pottery and related areas. An example is Haystack Mountain School of Crafts in Deer Isle, Maine. Each summer, this school offers several classes on working with clay lasting one to three weeks each. Some focus on wheel-thrown pottery, while others cover handbuilding techniques. Related topics such as painting ceramic objects are also offered.

Peters Valley Craft Center in Layton, New Jersey, is another school offering classes in ceramics. Typical summer workshop titles include:

Form, Function, and Surface

The Dimension of Color

Functional Pots

Raku Firing: Kilns and Glazes

Working craftspersons, teachers, students, and others interested in this area may wish to join the National Council on Education for the Ceramic Arts. This organization provides a forum for sharing information about the ceramic arts through publications, conferences, and member networking.

For more information:

National Council on Education for the Ceramic Arts
P.O. Box 1677
Bandon, OR 97411

Haystack Mountain School of Crafts
P.O. Box 518
Deer Isle, ME 04627

Peters Valley Craft Center
19 Kuhn Road
Layton, OH 07851

Floral Designer

"A thing of beauty is a joy forever," the poet John Keats noted. Of course, that was before the days of FTD! While flowers may not last forever, there is certainly no doubt that flowers bring joy as well as other desired effects. Well-designed floral arrangements can thrill brides, surprise spouses, comfort the sick, or convey a message of sympathy.

With the value people place on flowers, it is not surprising that the floral industry is a large and thriving one. Within this multifaceted business are not only jobs in sales, agriculture, and other areas, but also opportunities for those with an inclination toward crafts. Specifically, the job of floral designer offers great promise for people with an eye for beauty and a creative flair.

Floral designers have a wider range of career opportunities than do followers of some other crafts due to the immense popularity of flowers. This multibillion-dollar industry has room for independent floral designers or florists, those employed by retail flower shops, and various related workers including cut flower processors, salespersons, interior landscapers, and managers in retail or wholesale establishments.

Although on-the-job training is possible, most floral designers today receive some type of formal education. Many vocational schools, trade schools, and community colleges offer programs in floral design or the related areas of floriculture or horticulture. Some of these programs take two years to complete, while others can be finished in a year or less. A catalog of schools offering these programs is available from the Society of American Florists. A nearby community college or vocational school may also be a possibility if you would like to explore this career area.

Persons with disabilities may be interested in a special program which supports the hiring of the disabled in the horticulture field. This national referral network has placed over one thousand people in jobs in the floral industry and related fields. For more details, contact the American Horticultural Therapy Association.

For more information:

Society of American Florists
1601 Duke Street
Alexandria, VA 22314

Horticulture Hiring the Disabled
American Horticultural Therapy Association
9220 Wightman Road, Suite 300
Gaithersburg, MD 20879

Picture Framer

What if you're not the most artistic person in the world, but the idea of a crafts career appeals to you? One occupation worth considering is that of professional picture framer. This is not to say that picture framers lack talent; on the contrary, this craft provides much in the way of creative challenge. On the other hand, almost anyone can take a shot at this field. The main requirements are patience and enthusiasm. An eye for proportion is also helpful, as is an appreciation for color, contrast, and texture. And just as it is with virtually every craft area, the ability to work with your hands is needed. Most people can develop their abilities in these areas, so career possibilities are wide open in this field.

What do picture framers do? That may sound like a silly question. They frame pictures, of course! But actually, the job is more complex than might seem at first glance. It involves choosing materials, making special borders called mats (also spelled *matts* or *mattes*), assembling frames, cutting glass, and handling other tasks necessary for protecting and displaying pictures. These pictures could be photographs, paintings, or drawings. Picture framers also work with a wide range of other items including diplomas, certificates, rare documents, maps, newspaper clippings, collages, and needlecraft. Framers also work with objects that are not as flat as pictures and documents. For example, they might construct frameworks or displays for coin collections, arrowheads, or medallions.

The world of picture framing goes hand in hand with that of the visual arts. Some painters, for instance, learn to make their own frames, then go on to provide this service for others. In the process, they develop skills in a second field which enhances their ability to produce income.

Some picture framers build working relationships with artists in which they not only provide frames, but also help market the finished product. They might operate an art gallery as an adjunct to their framing services.

Many picture framers are self-employed or operate their own small businesses. Others work for art galleries, museums, or private companies that manufacture frames.

Running a framing shop can be one of the most promising ways to combine a crafts-related career with a small business that appeals to a broad segment of the public. These shops serve not just the artistic community, but everyone from hobbyists to doting grandparents anxious to display huge color photos of the smartest grandchildren in the universe. As such, they provide a way for the competent framer to build and operate a successful business.

Frame shops and galleries represent one of the best ways to get started in this field. Here, experienced framers are sometimes willing to train a part-time employee or apprentice. Working with an experienced picture framer can provide perhaps the best introduction to the craft.

Another approach is to take classes or seminars on picture framing, to read books on the subject, or to view videotapes on basic framing techniques. All of these are available through the Professional Picture Framers Association (PPFA), an organization with seven thousand American and Canadian members. It provides a variety of services of interest to anyone committed to picture framing as a professional endeavor.

Newcomers to the field will be especially interested in instructional opportunities offered through the association. These include seminars offered throughout the United States and Canada which are open to nonmembers as well as PPFA members. Examples of seminar topics include:

Beginning Mat Cutting

Object Box Framing

Conservation Framing

Gallery Presentation and Display

Also of special interest is an association "bookstore" which provides books and training videos. Not only are they easily ordered by mail, telephone, or fax machines, but their prices are discounted for members. Examples of videotapes include "The Basics of Picture Framing" and "The Basics of Mat Cutting and Decoration," both by Vivian Kistler, as well as other tapes on topics ranging from conservation framing to French matting.

Another appealing service is a special program for certifying professional picture framers. This provides a helpful way to recognize professional skills.

For more information:

Professional Picture Framers Association
    4305 Sarellen Road
    Richmond, VA 23231
    (800) 832-PPFA (U.S.)
    (800) 833-PPFA (Canada)

Candle Maker

A craft area that has been making something of a comeback in recent years is candle making. Used purely for decoration or burned as an alternative to modern electric lights, candles are popular items with people from a variety of backgrounds.

"For romantics, candles are always in," says Chris Saunders, a Virginia candle maker. He makes candles of various sizes and configurations, selling them at crafts fairs and by consignment in shops.

"Candles are great for people who believe in a return to the basics," Saunders says. "You can produce them in quantity, or you can consider each one a work of art."

To learn about the craft, Saunders suggests contacting a working craftsperson and learning firsthand. Individual practice and experimentation are essential. Although there is plenty of room for creativity, this area is one where beginners can learn quickly.

Working candle makers and others interested in the field belong to the International Guild of Candle Artisans. This group produces a newsletter called *The Candlelighter,* sponsors conferences, and even operates a hot line to provide tips on problems candle makers encounter in their work. Also of note are workshops the group holds which feature instruction in candle making techniques.

For more information:

International Guild of Candle Artisans
1305 Walker NW, No. 4102
Grand Rapids, MI 49504

Related Careers

Along with the careers profiled earlier, a wide range of occupations deal with glass, pottery, or other materials discussed in this chapter. Following is a brief listing of some of them.

Fused Glass Artists form and shape glass in kilns. They construct everything from cups and bowls to abstract sculptures.

GLAZIERS cut and install window glass. While this work falls more within the area of construction than that of handicrafts, it requires skill and precision akin to that needed by other craftspersons who work with glass.

GLASS DECORATORS use painting or other techniques to add designs to glass products. This may be done by hand or through automated processes.

PORCELAIN WARE DESIGNERS create the designs that other workers follow in producing dishware and related products. Their work revolves more around the creation of new designs than the actual production of pieces in quantity.

OPTICAL TECHNICIANS and others who work with optical products create lenses, optical mirrors, and related objects. This work can range from the routine production of eyeglass lenses to highly individualized work such as grinding and polishing lenses or mirrors for telescopes.

Further Reading

Birks, Tony. Pottery. Lark Books, 1988.

Cameron, Elizabeth, and Phillipa Lewis. Potters on Pottery. St. Martin's Press, 1976.

Duthie, Arthur. Decorative Glass Processes. Dover Publications, 1982.

Eaton, Connie. Suncatchers Stained Glass Pattern Book. Dover Publications, 1987.

Hasluck, Paul, ed. Traditional Glassworking Techniques. Dover Publications, 1988.

Hoyt, Homer. Glassblowing: An Introduction to Solid and Blown Glass Sculpturing. Crafts and Arts Publishing Company, 1990.

Kenny, John B. The Complete Book of Pottery Making. Chilton Books, 1976.

McDonell, James. Stained Glass Craft Made Simple: Step-by-Step Instructions Using the Modern Copper-Foil Method. Dover Publications, 1985.

Norman, Barbara. Engraving and Decorating Glass: Methods and Techniques. Dover Publications, 1987.

Leather and Lace

Are you passionate about leather? After all, you don't need to be a biker to appreciate the soft feel and rich smell of new leather. Or are you more of a soft-fabric type? The delicate beauty of handcrafted textiles can be hard to beat.

Whatever your preferences, at least one craft area addresses them. In fact, the creation of clothing, rugs, quilts, and other items provides one of the more diverse of existing craft areas. Craftspersons who can sew, weave, design clothing, or perform related work often find substantial demand for their products. By the same token, the crafty person can find many rewards by working in this area.

Leather Artisan

Craftspersons who work with leather provide products that are useful, long-lasting, and often quite attractive. In an age dominated by synthetic materials and mass-produced clothing, they appeal to the growing popularity of handmade, individualized items.

Gregory Neal of Chase City, Virginia, is an example of a successful craftsperson in this field. Originally an electrical contractor, he started working with leather on a part-time basis. As his business grew, he made the transition to full-time artisan.

"I design, make, and sell all types of leather products," he notes, citing customers ranging from Kmart to individuals who frequent crafts fairs. He has based his company in a forty-by-forty-foot shop building, where he makes wallets, belts, novelty items, and other leather goods.

"To make a go of it, you have to come up with things lots of people will buy," he says. As an example, he points to the leather rifle cases which have become a popular item.

Neal also finds that a willingness to travel is helpful. He travels to crafts fairs and stores throughout the eastern United States, spending the entire month of January in Florida and attending leather conventions in New York during warm-weather months.

"It's great being your own boss, and the traveling is interesting," Neal says. "You do have to invest money in special equipment as well as leather itself. But it can be worth it."

Neal and others who work with leather often find that customers are highly receptive to the chance to own handcrafted products. Since leather is widely used by both men and women, the market for finely crafted goods is a large one.

As with any craft, there are some shortcomings. One is that leather is a rather expensive raw material, thus items that are made but not sold can tie up a good deal of money. Another occasional problem is resentment by some environmentalists. Since leather comes from the hides of cows and a variety of more exotic animals, those who work with leather can become targets of environmental activists. This situation is generally not as controversial as it is with fur, but it can come up. Artisans who work with leather generally learn noncombative responses to use if criticized about this issue.

Some working craftspersons in this field belong to national groups of those with similar interests. For more information, contact:

International Federation of Leather Guilds
P.O. Box 102
Arcadia, IN 46030

Leathercraft Guild
P.O. Box 734
Artesia, CA 90701

Weaver

If you want to stick with a traditional craft, it would be hard to beat weaving. Weavers carry on a practice that has continued throughout the world for thousands of years. Today's weavers provide an alternative to the high-volume, industrialized processes with which most cloth-based materials are produced. The beautiful patterns of a handwoven tapestry, for example, stand in stark contrast to the mass-produced effect created by assembly-line production methods.

For those with the right combination of skill and patience, weaving can provide a productive career area. The work of accomplished weavers is seen not just as an alternative way of making rugs or other functional items, but also as the creation of highly prized works of art.

Robert Loewe teaches weaving at Great Divide Weaving School in Divide, Colorado. While many of his students take on weaving as a hobby, some have gone on to make it a career. "I think it takes vision, determination, and guts," he says. "Having simple tastes helps."

At this school, located in a beautiful, rustic site in the Rockies, students learn the basics of weaving in one or two weeks of intensive instruction. Both beginners and those with some previous experience may enroll. Students are limited to three per class, and each student receives a great deal of individualized instruction.

Learning the basics of weaving at the school means working on a two-harness loom to create a rug or tapestry. Students first choose the colors with which they plan to work and decide which weaving techniques they would like to master. They study drawings of weaving techniques, learn to use the loom, and begin working on a weaving project, which normally takes three days to complete. They then work on one or more additional weaving projects (depending on whether they enroll for six days or twelve), and some also learn how to dye wool.

The downside of weaving, from a career viewpoint, is that it is difficult to be productive enough to create and sell enough pieces to earn a living, given the methodical nature of the weaving process. This can be done, however, thanks not just to individual productivity, but also to the value many customers place in handwoven material. As with many other products in the arts and crafts, the work of an accomplished weaver can fetch excellent prices. Thus with skill and persistence, it is possible to make weaving a part-time or full-time occupation.

Robert Loewe of the Great Divide School serves as a good example of success in this area. He has been a full-time weaver for more than fifteen years and has sold over 250 weavings. Like many other successful craftspersons, he has combined creative work with teaching.

Weavings of first-rate craftspersons such as Loewe are popular items for decorating offices, government buildings, and homes. Weavers sell their products through galleries, arts and crafts fairs, special arrangements with merchandisers, and their own marketing efforts.

A good source of information about weaving is the Handweavers Guild of America. A local fine arts center, crafts center, or college continuing education program may also provide classes or put you in touch with accomplished weavers.

For more information:

Handweavers Guild of America
   120 Mountain Avenue
   Bloomfield, CT 06002

Great Divide Weaving School
   Box W
   Divide, CO 80814-9018

Quilter

Some craft areas hold special appeal because they continue the legacy of the past. As with weaving, this is certainly true of quilting, one of the most popular of craft areas. The days of the quilting bee may be virtually over, but people of all ages still love the unique appeal of quilted materials.

While the major item of interest in the field is probably the traditional quilt to be used as a bed covering, those skilled in crafting produce a variety of other materials. Examples include place mats, runners, coasters, table centers, and various sizes of wall hangings.

Making quilts by hand takes great patience. At the same time, the finished work is often coveted by customers and may fetch high prices. From a business viewpoint, the difficulty is reconciling the many hours it takes to produce fine work with the need to keep costs low enough for customers to afford.

An alternative to making quilts entirely by hand is machine quilting. This process is considerably faster but one that still can produce beautiful work. Some quilters learn both processes to increase their capacity while not abandoning traditional methods.

To learn more about quilting, consult one of the many books available on the subject (several are listed at the end of this chapter). Or take a class or talk with someone in your area who is active in quilting.

Doll Maker

Another very popular craft area is making dolls. This is an area dear to the hearts of a surprisingly large number of people. Dolls are *not* just for children, if this craft is any indicator. To the contrary, the work of doll makers is of interest to a wide range of customers including collectors, parents, grandparents, and doll enthusiasts of all ages.

Those who make dolls work with a wide range of materials. Some create finely wrought figures of porcelain. Some doll makers use wood, plastic, or other durable materials. Still others fashion dolls out of cloth, corn cobs, or whatever else might work. Doll makers also specialize in a variety of subjects including clowns, mechanical dolls, and dolls dressed in period costumes.

A good source of information about doll making is the Doll Artisan Guild, headquartered in Oneonta, New York. Members of this organization receive six issues per year of *The Doll Artisan* (a magazine that includes pull-out worksheets for doll-making projects), enjoy manufacturer's discounts, and compete for awards based on their work. The group also sponsors conventions, doll-making seminars, and opportunities to become certified at several levels of ability.

Several other groups also serve the needs of doll makers. For more information:

Doll Artisan Guild
  35 Main Street
  P.O. Box 1113
  Oneonta, NY 13820-1113

International Foundation of Doll Makers
  P.O. Box 14438
  Ft. Worth, TX 76117

International Doll Makers Association
  25203 Cathedral
  Redford, MN 48239

Basket Maker

Basket makers also practice a craft that goes back thousands of years. Remember the story of Moses floating at the edge of the Nile River? The boat holding the infant was actually a basket.

Throughout history, craftspersons from almost every culture have made and used baskets. Today's basket makers use the same kinds of techniques that have existed for centuries, with the added benefit of new raw materials, paints, and other coverings. Just some of the materials used to make baskets include strips of wood or bark, grass, and various fibers ranging from wool and cotton to synthetic fibers. The major attributes needed to produce baskets of good quality are patience, steady hands, and skill built up through practice.

The Arrowmont School of Arts and Crafts in Gatlinburg, Tennessee is one school which teaches classes in basket making. For example, one course called Rattan Wicker Basketry covers the construction of traditional wicker baskets using rattan—the stems of any of several climbing palms. Topics of discussion include wicker weaves, making lids and handles, and dealing with color.

Many other schools also offer seminars or short courses in basketry. Check with a nearby community college or adult education program to identify available courses in your area.

For more information:

Arrowmont School of Arts and Crafts
P.O. Box 567
Gatlinburg, TN 37738

Fashion Designer

A major career area for people with the right artistic bent is the design of dresses and other clothing. This can range from a home-based business, in which you design and sew clothing for customers within your own community, to working as a designer for a major apparel firm.

Clothing design offers a wide range of opportunities for part-time or full-time employment. Just some examples of career possibilities in this area are as follows:

- Designing wedding gowns for a clothing manufacturer
- Designing and creating wedding gowns through your own home-based business
- Designing costumes for plays, movies, or television
- Providing custom dress design services for department stores or boutiques
- Operating your own tailoring business
- Providing customized tailoring services for men's clothing stores or department stores
- Designing and setting up window displays for department stores or clothing stores
- Working as a milliner for a hat company
- Providing alteration services for cleaners, clothing stores, or other establishments
- Specializing in designing or producing clothing for specialized groups such as infants or small children

Fashion design or clothing design is an area where although it is possible to pursue a career based on your own talent and experimentation, it is often helpful to pursue some type of specialized training. One approach is to work as an apprentice or assistant to an experienced designer. Another is to enroll in classes offered by a school that offers fashion design or related programs.

An example is the Clarissa School of Fashion Design in Pittsburgh. Here, students may earn a two-year associate degree in either apparel technology or fashion design. They take courses such as the following:

Swatch-Construction Techniques I and II

Dressmaking I, II, and III

Patternmaking I, II, and III

Textiles

Fashion Illustration

Fashion Writing

Color and Line

Personal Improvement

Retail and Business Math

Merchandising

Fashion Past and Present

Fashion Advertising and Sales Promotion

Pattern Grading

Consumer Management

Apparel Design I and II

Women's Tailoring

Draping I and II

Visual Display

Clothing and Society

Professional Orientation and Portfolio Design

Do you have to take such courses? Not necessarily, but obviously a job applicant with such training will have an advantage over one who has no special training in fashion design. On the other hand, many of the concepts taught in formal courses can be picked up through related job experience. If you are lucky enough to sign on with an experienced designer, or if you start out working alone but do plenty of reading, studying, and practicing in the field, it is possible to get started in fashion design without a great deal of formal instruction.

A career in fashion design has its pros and cons. On the negative side, this is an extremely competitive field. On the positive side, designing new fashions offers the potential of business success along with the fun of creating new designs. This is not a field for everyone, but it is one that can be highly rewarding for the right crafty person.

Bookbinder

The skills of sewing and cutting are not confined to making clothes, baskets, or other household items. A related but very different area is the binding of books. With all the high-tech equipment used in today's publishing industry, you might think that bookbinding is an outdated craft. Not true!

Books are fragile. Older volumes may begin to fall apart due to extensive use, age, or a combination of the two. Yet they may be worth saving. In fact, many old books are considered valuable by collectors, professors, libraries, and others. In restructuring books, bookbinders extend the useful life of the volumes. In addition, newly published books targeted to limited audiences may require handbinding instead of the mass-production techniques of the latest best seller. As a result of demands for both kinds of work, a continuing need exists for skilled bookbinders.

Employers of bookbinders include binderies, university publishers and libraries, and custom shops specializing in bookbinding, publishing, or related services. Some bookbinders also go the small business route and operate their own businesses.

Due to the specialized nature of the work, some type of training is necessary to get started in this field. Some schools offer continuing education classes or summer workshops in bookbinding, and a few offer more extensive training.

A school offering a full-fledged program in this field is North Bennet Street School in Boston. Here, students learn bookbinding through a two-year program which includes training in the unique vocabulary and techniques of bookbinding, followed by intensive hands-on experience in repairing books from the nineteenth and twentieth centuries as well as working with new books. Students attend small classes (average class size is twelve) for forty weeks each year, meeting daily from 8:00 a.m. to 2:00 p.m. Along with classroom instruction, they go on field trips and attend special lectures and demonstrations. The main component of the program, though, is extensive bench work.

If you are unable to attend a school of this type, it may be possible to learn bookbinding through an arrangement with an experienced craftsperson. Through a formal apprenticeship or informal, on-the-job training, a diligent worker can learn the techniques of this field. To succeed, you will need patience, good hand-eye coordination, and other skills not unlike those of many other craft areas. A love of books is also a great asset. In fact, a dedicated bookbinder will regard books the way a jeweler treasures diamonds. With a deep respect for the value of books, an eye for beauty, and a willingness to work patiently, skilled bookbinders provide important work.

For more information:

North Bennet Street School
39 North Bennet Street
Boston, MA 02113

Book Manufacturers Institute
111 Prospect
Stamford, CT 06901

Related Careers

Occupations related to those discussed in this chapter include the following:

FUR DESIGNERS create designs for coats, hats, and other items made of animal fur. Their work is similar to that of fashion designers but with a more narrow range of working materials.

LACE AND TEXTILE RESTORERS work primarily for museums. They repair and restore old clothing, linens, and other related items of historical value.

GIFT WRAPPERS work primarily for retail stores but may also operate their own businesses. They use skills not greatly different from those of designers. They choose color combinations and designs and wrap packages as creatively as possible.

MANNEQUIN DECORATORS create store displays by dressing and posing mannequins. They exercise creativity in trying to catch the attention of customers by coming up with interesting or attractive clothing combinations.

FURNITURE UPHOLSTERERS add the fabric coverings to the frameworks of sofas, chairs, and other types of furniture. Some specialize in working with new furniture while others focus on reupholstering older furniture.

SADDLERS perform the highly specialized job of making or repairing saddles used in riding horses. They may also sell saddles made by others. Some saddlers also make related products such as stirrups or reins; the latter work can also be performed by harness makers.

Further Reading

Books

Brown, Rachel. *The Weaving, Spinning and Dyeing Book*. Alfred A, Knopf, 1983.
Cherry, Raymond. *Leathercrafting: Procedures and Projects*. Glencoe Publishing, 1979.
Christopher, Catherine. *Complete Book of Doll Making and Collecting*. Dover, 1970.

Frank, Agnes, and Linda Stokes. *Quilting for Beginners: Patchwork and Applique Projects for All Ages*. Sterling Publishing, 1990.

Garnes, Jane E. *The Complete Handbook of Leathercrafting*. Krieger Publishing, 1986.

Green, Caroline. *Quilting*. Sterling Publishing, 1990.

Groneman, Chris. *Leather Tooling and Carving*. Dover, 1974.

Harvey, Virginia. *The Techniques of Basketry*. University of Washington Press, 1986.

Magazines

Fiberarts
50 College Street
Asheville, NC 28801

Handwoven and *Spin-Off*
Interweave Press
201 East 4th Street
Loveland, CO 80537

Heddle Magazine
P.O. Box 1906
Bracebridge, Ontario
P1L 1V8 Canada

Miniature Quilts and *Traditional Quiltworks*
Chitra Publications
2 Public Avenue
Montrose, PA 18801

Needlepoint Plus
1320 Galaxy Way
Concord, CA 94520

Sew News
PJS Publications
P.O. Box 1790
Peoria, IL 61656

Shuttle Spindle & Dyepot
120 Mountain Road
Bloomfield, CT 06002

Traditional Quilter
MSC Publishing Company
243 Newton-Sparta Road
Newton, NJ 07860

CHAPTER SIX

Graphic Details

N
o discussion of craft careers would be complete without a look at the graphic arts. Creating and producing lettering, drawings, and other graphic images is an area rich in possibilities for the crafty person.

Do you enjoy drawing? Painting? Coming up with visual images that in a single glance convey more than a page of words? If so, one of the following careers may be just right for you.

Craft Painter

The distinction between artist and craftsperson is a fuzzy one. In the area of painting, someone who produces lifelike oil paintings of museum quality would probably be called an artist. Someone else who adds painted illustrations to functional objects would probably be called a craftsperson. For example, one craft technique is painting on the blades of handsaws. Another is applying likenesses of birds or forest animals to slabs of rough wood.

Marilyn Stacey of Ferrisburg, Vermont, specializes in painting roof slates. Not only is slate one of Vermont's most famous products, but the smooth, multicolored stone was once a popular form of roofing in the state. By making decorative pieces from old slates once used for roofing, Stacey appeals to tourists who want to acquire a keepsake related to Vermont as well as to residents who covet a token of the past. At the same time, slate makes an attractive material for wall hangings, desk pieces, or plaques.

The secret to making it in a craft occupation, according to Stacey, is hard work. "You have to be a self-disciplined person," she notes. "I work at least forty hours most weeks, and sometimes more than that. I have to work especially hard in the winter to build up inventory for sales in the spring and summer."

Stacey creates wall hangings, clocks, trivets, spoon racks, refrigerator magnets, and desk nameblocks, among other items. On their surfaces, she paints images of flowers, wildlife, farm animals, barns, covered bridges, and other pastoral objects.

In the course of her work, she avoids any type of mass production or repetition. Instead, she constantly tries to come up with new designs.

"As a craftsperson, you need to change and grow," she notes. "It's important to keep the element of creativity alive."

Other craft painters work with a variety of media. Many sell their works at crafts fairs or by word of mouth. Some combine their craft with teaching, running frame shops, or pursuing other crafts.

An advantage of craft painting is that no special training is necessary. Although classes in painting or drawing can be helpful, anyone who has basic abilities in drawing or painting and who can develop products of respectable quality might find this craft of interest.

Sign Painter

If work as a sign painter does not appeal to you, then consider sign writing. Actually, both terms refer to the same thing! Sign painters (or sign writers, if you prefer) design and apply lettering and graphic designs for use in various kinds of signs. They produce billboards, posters, door and window signs, and other types of messages. Sign painting can provide several options for the person interested in this area. It can be the major product of a small business or one of many such services provided by a full-service graphics or printing establishment. Sign painters thus can work on their own as self-employed craftspersons or as employees of graphics firms, outdoor advertising companies, full-service ad agencies, or other types of employers.

Traditionally, the work of sign painters has been done by hand. A typical example would be the application of a person's name on the outside of an office's glass door. Using a brush and paint, the sign painter would carefully add the appropriate lettering. As technology changes, however, some of this work will be accomplished through the use of lettering machines or computerized processes. Sign writers might also employ skills ranging from screen printing to working with gold or silver leaf.

Calligrapher

If you have ever spotted words such as "whereas" or "wherefore" in a modern-day document, or the abbreviation "R.S.V.P." in an invitation, chances are you have seen the work of a calligrapher. Such wording is the staple of formal resolutions, invitations, and similar printed materials.

Calligraphers produce handlettered material for situations in which the appearance of the finished product is of special importance. Invitations, nameplates, resolutions, diplomas, and certificates of merit are just a few examples. In documents such as these, it is the job of the calligrapher to provide attractive lettering, often with the goal of simulating the old-fashioned lettering used in the days before typewriting (let alone word processing) was commonplace.

A job as a calligrapher is likely to be a part-time one, or else a component of a more broad-based career which includes other types of graphic services. By its very nature, calligraphy is a painstakingly slow process, and it is difficult to consistently produce enough finished work to support a full-fledged career. However, some people do succeed at making it a full-time occupation. They provide services to businesses, government agencies, nonprofit organizations, and individuals.

For the right person, calligraphy can provide highly satisfying work which differs greatly from more mainstream careers. It combines the creativity of the artist with the precision of the craft practitioner. In fact, the term *calligraphy* can be roughly translated from its Greek origins as "beautiful writing." This element of beauty makes calligraphy stand out from many other occupations.

Working alone or in collaboration with a client, the calligrapher first chooses the style of lettering to be used in any given project. Then, he or she carefully draws each letter using special pens designed to transfer an even flow of ink onto the paper.

A representative task would consist of taking a stack of printed certificates developed to honor a group of employees or volunteers, and one by one writing in the names of the individual recipients. Other typical projects would be producing corporate logos, lettering invitations to special events, or developing place cards for formal dinners.

Some calligraphers go beyond basic lettering to produce artistic works. These can include unusual renditions of lettering in which the letters themselves become a creative art form. Another approach is to add drawings to lettering, producing a combined art form akin to the illustrated manuscripts introduced in medieval times.

Most calligraphers learn their craft through a combination of instruction and individual practice. The instructional end might consist of a class or two offered by a community college, a workshop presented during a summer camp or arts and crafts festival, or classes offered through a public school system's community education program. Or it might be based on lessons taken from an experienced calligrapher. Still another alternative is simply consulting books about calligraphy and mastering it independently.

Whatever the means of initial instruction, the bulk of the learning process will consist of practicing the appropriate techniques. Like learning to play the piano or successfully shooting free throws in basketball, learning calligraphy means practice, practice, and more practice. Once the basics of this demanding craft have been mastered, the accomplished calligrapher possesses an ability few others can duplicate, thus demands for the calligrapher's work can be high.

With the advent of desktop publishing, the special appeal of calligraphy faces a serious challenge. With the right computer software and a sophisticated printer, an otherwise untrained person can produce work that mimics hand lettering in a fraction of the time needed for traditional calligraphy. With a choice of type styles and the ability to correct mistakes almost instantly, any skilled computer user can produce material that rivals that of the accomplished calligrapher. Accordingly, some people think that calligraphy is doomed to become an obsolete field. Others disagree. They contend that the appeal of work done by hand may actually increase, serving as one counterpoint to an increasingly depersonalized, highly technological society. If this is true, then people will always be willing to pay a premium for the beautiful work that skilled calligraphers are able to produce.

For more information:

Society for Calligraphy
P.O. Box 64174
Los Angeles, CA 90064

Washington Calligraphers Guild
P.O. Box 3688
Merrifield, VA 22116-3688

Greeting Card Illustrator

When was the last time you bought a greeting card? Were you impressed with the number and variety of cards available? The fact is, people purchase millions of greeting cards every year. While some consist only of verbal messages, many others include drawings or other illustrations. These cards would not be possible without the work of greeting card illustrators.

Illustrators fill several types of roles in the greeting card industry. Some work exclusively as illustrators for large companies that specialize in greeting cards. Others work in smaller companies. Some work independently of any one company, either free-lancing as illustrators or collaborating with writers to produce their own line of cards. Some individuals who are talented at both art and writing may combine the two functions, running their own small business which includes producing and marketing cards.

Illustrators of greeting cards work in much the same way as do other illustrators. Most of their time is spent at drawing boards or computer consoles. Those who work as full-time employees of greeting card companies may have their own offices or designated work spaces. Illustrators who own their own businesses may rent office space or work out of their home.

As with other types of illustrators, this work involves a collaborative process. Unless the illustrator is also a writer, the creative process involves responding to written work produced by a writer or concept specialist. Typically, the illustrator reads written copy and then comes up with one or more possible illustrations, usually in the form of rough sketches. Then an editor, writer, or other members of a work group review the drafts, possibly suggest changes, and make a selection. The illustrator then follows up by producing the finished illustration.

In some cases, illustrations may be discussed in advance so that a writer or editor can explain what is desired. In other instances, it is up to the illustrator to originate ideas. Occasionally, the process may be reversed, with the illustrator initiating an idea and a writer coming up with wording to match it.

What are the best features about a career in illustrating greeting cards? One is the variety involved. Some greeting cards are serious. Others are humorous. They may be directed at men, women, children, graduates, sick people, lovers, or any of dozens of other target groups. Illustrators may produce cartoonlike drawings, landscapes, or holiday scenes. To appeal to buyers, there is always the demand to come up with something new. As a result, the work offers a great deal of variety and a dominant spirit of creativity.

Another favorable point is the popularity of greeting cards. Unlike some types of craftspersons who may see limited demand for their work, illustrators of greeting cards help provide a product that is in great demand as a mainstream commodity. Only a small percentage of the population will ever buy a handwoven rug, for instance. But check out the card section of the nearest Wal-Mart the day before Mother's Day and you will see a good example of the universal appeal of greeting cards!

While there are no specific educational requirements for working in this field, most greeting card companies prefer to employ people with a college or trade-school education in graphic design, art, or a related field. Experience in computer graphics may also be required. Free-lancers or those who start their own businesses may set their own requirements. Certainly, they need polished skills in drawing, painting, and other related areas. To impress potential employers or clients, a portfolio if drawings or other work may be required.

Experienced illustrators who have specialized in greeting cards can easily make the transition to other related jobs should they desire. Their skills can be applied to positions as graphic artists, technical illustrators, or other occupations with similar demands.

A helpful organization for people interested in this field is the Greeting Card Creative Network, located in Washington, D.C. Not only does this group sponsor conferences and seminars on various aspects of the industry, but it also publishes a market list which covers the needs of specific publishers and tips on packaging submissions. It also provides newsletters and other publications, instructional tapes, consulting referrals, and a free listing for members in a talent directory sent to more than nine hundred greeting card publishers in the United States.

For more information:

Greeting Card Creative Network
1200 G Street NW, Suite 760
Washington, DC 20005

Cartoonist

One of the most individualistic of all careers is that of cartoonist. In a way, being a cartoonist is like being a novelist, poet, or essayist. The work is expressive, original, and creative. Usually it comes not as some externally mandated task, such as the work of an illustrator, but rather from the imagination of the artist. For example, consider the work of famous cartoonists such as Gary Larson, the creator of the zany series "The Far Side," or of Charles Schultz, who has become wealthy by creating Snoopy and all the "Peanuts" gang.

An overview of career possibilities for cartoonists contains both good news and bad news. The good news is that cartoonists can enjoy wonderful, stimulating careers. They do enjoyable work which if printed in newspapers or magazines, also can be enjoyed by thousands or even millions of people.

The bad news is that relatively few people actually succeed at making a full-time, paying occupation of drawing cartoons. Of course, some people *do* make this their profession, and there will always be room for more, so this is still a career worth considering for those who are both talented and persistent.

While the daily comic pages in newspapers might be the first thing that comes to mind when one considers the work of cartoonists, the field has other possibilities. For example, political cartoons, found on most editorial pages, represent a specialty of their own. Many magazines also publish cartoons, most of which are designed to stand alone rather than be part of a series. Cartoonists are also employed by the motion picture industry and by publishers of comic books.

One way to get started in this field is to study art in a college or art school program and make cartooning a major emphasis of class projects and other efforts. The work produced then can become part of a portfolio to show to prospective employers.

Another approach is to pursue cartooning on a free-lance basis. Here, the best way may be to start small by developing a regular cartoon feature for a school paper or neighborhood newspaper, then using that experience to approach a larger newspaper—or even better, regional or national syndicates. Individual cartoons also can be submitted to magazines that consider free-lance submissions of cartoons. You can find more information about places to sell cartoons in the book *Humor and Cartoon Markets,* published annually by Writer's Digest Books (1507 Dana Avenue, Cincinnati, OH 45207).

For more information about cartooning:

Graphic Artists Guild
    11 W. 20th Street
    New York, NY 10011

Museum of Cartoon Art
    Comly Avenue
    Rye Brook, NY 10573

Cartoon Art Museum
    665 Third Street
    San Francisco, CA 94107

Medical Illustrator

Take one part art and one part science, and the result is an important yet unusual craft: medical illustration.

If you have ever glanced through an encyclopedia or killed time in a doctor's examining room by studying wall posters with their drawings of various parts of the human body, you have seen firsthand the work of medical illustrators. Men and women who hold jobs in this field constitute a small but vital profession. They render detailed drawings of the human anatomy for use in books, slides, videotapes, and other media. These materials are used for science classes, medical school classes, and other instructional purposes.

The work of medical illustrators covers not just the way organs or other body parts look, but also how they function. For example, an illustrator may draw a series of pictures of white blood cells to show how they attack and kill invading bacteria. Illustrators may also develop drawings and diagrams of medical processes. For instance, an illustrator might work closely with a surgeon who has developed a new surgical technique. The illustrator develops drawings which show, on a step-by-step basis, how the surgery is conducted. The finished drawings can then be used to help medical students or practicing surgeons learn the surgery.

The old adage "one picture is worth a thousand words" certainly holds true in this field. A carefully rendered medical illustration can hold tremendous value for those who must master complex concepts and techniques.

Because of its specialized nature, this field requires advanced training. Typically, this consists of a master's degree in medical illustration completed after a bachelor's degree has been earned in art or a scientific field such as biology, anatomy, or zoology.

Only a few schools offer such programs. Those accredited by the American Medical Association's Committee on Allied Health Education and Accreditation (CAHEA) are as follows:

Colorado State University
Fort Collins, CO 80523

The Medical College of Georgia
Augusta, GA 30912-0300

University of Illinois at Chicago
1919 West Taylor Street
Chicago, IL 60612

The Johns Hopkins School of Medicine
1830 E. Monument Street, Suite 7000
Baltimore, MD 21205

The University of Michigan
North Brewery, 1327 Jones Drive
Ann Arbor, MI 48109-1897

The University of Texas Southwestern Medical Center at Dallas
P.O. Box 46668, Exchange Park
Dallas, TX 75245

A Canadian program is located at:

University of Toronto
256 McCaul Street
Toronto, Ontario,
M5T 1W5, Canada

The Association of Medical Illustrators provides publications and other membership services, including some funding for scholarships, summer internship programs, and certification programs. For more information:

Association of Medical Illustrators
1819 Peachtree Street N.E.
Suite 560
Atlanta, GA 30309

Book and Magazine Illustrator

If medical illustration seems too specialized for your interests, keep in mind that there is always a demand for those who can serve as general illustrators for books, magazines, and other publications. Any time you pick up a book or magazine, chances are you will see drawings, paintings, or other illustrations.

Some illustrators are employed as full-time staffers by book publishing companies or magazine publishers. Their usual role involves a three-step process:

1. Reading written material developed by a writer or editor.

2. Coming up with a drawing or other illustration which enhances or illuminates a key concept.

3. Revising illustrations in response to suggestions by editors.

Illustrators who are not employed on a full-time or permanent basis work as free-lancers. In this case, the basic tasks performed are the same as for full-time staffers, but the illustrators work out of their own studios, typically in their homes. In addition, their relationships with editors differ. They may work for any number of magazines or publishing companies at any given time. Too, a good portion of their work may be spent on business details as opposed to the actual work of illustration. Typical such tasks include contacting editors or art directors to drum up business, packing drawings and sending them by mail or delivery service, and keeping track of invoices, payments, and so forth. In some cases, illustrators may collaborate with writers to develop children's books or other projects before they are submitted to publishing companies. More often, their work is done after a manuscript has been written and scheduled for publication.

To succeed in this field, illustrators need the ability to produce clear, recognizable drawings, paintings, or graphic designs. They must work quickly enough to meet deadlines. Another helpful trait is the ability to read perceptively, since the crux of their work is enhancing the written word.

Training options vary. Most illustrators study commercial art or some other type of art in trade schools, art schools, community colleges, or universities. Before landing jobs or free-lance assignments, they usually develop portfolios which include samples of their work.

Cartographer

Cartographers design and produce maps. Their work combines the elements of science with the artistic work of drawing and illustrating. Some positions in this field emphasize the former, while others include the graphic skills needed for the production and printing of maps.

Most cartographers study geography at the college level. Some students focus on research or mapping sciences such as the interpretation of satellite photos. Others, whose work would be more interesting to crafty people, specialize in typography or drawing. Most cartographers use both hand duplication and computer programs to produce maps and their components. As in other fields, the use of computers is becoming an increasingly important part of the overall work of those involved in cartography.

The American Congress on Surveying and Mapping is a major organization whose membership includes those interested in cartography. Among other services, this group provides a variety of publications related to cartography.

For more information:

American Congress on Surveying and Mapping
    5410 Grosvenor Lane
    Bethesda, MD 20814
    (301) 493-0200

Other Graphics Jobs

This chapter has provided an overview of several job areas of possible interest to crafty people. Other related job titles include the following:

COMMERCIAL ARTISTS play a generalist's role. They use artistic skills to produce work requested by clients. They may produce anything from logos to newspaper ads. More and more, their work is done by computer rather than by hand. Commercial artists may also be known as graphic designers.

DESKTOP PUBLISHERS use computers to produce printed works. While some emphasize the writing aspect of this work, others concentrate on the amazing array of graphic images which can be produced with desktop publishing software.

GLASS DECORATORS take glass objects and add their own decorations through painting or other techniques. A similar job is performed by pottery decorators.

FASHION ARTISTS specialize in creating graphic designs of clothing and related items. They may create sketches of new designs based on descriptions provided by fashion designers, or perhaps re-create existing pieces for use in catalogs or ads.

PAINTING RESTORERS take old or damaged paintings and painstakingly restore them as closely as possible to their original quality. Their work requires both artistic skill and the knowledge of special techniques for duplicating styles and materials used in earlier times.

PHOTOGRAPH RETOUCHERS use artistic skills to improve the quality of photographs. They remove or cover blemishes and add attractive touches to make photos more appealing.

PRINTERS perform a variety of tasks related to the reproduction of written and graphic materials. In some cases, such as in small print shops, their work may include elements of graphic art and design.

TATOO ARTISTS are perhaps the only craftspersons who apply their work onto *people* rather than paper, canvas, or other inanimate materials. With the health risks now identified with tatooing, some who work in this area are beginning to adopt methods more akin to painting than traditional invasive techniques. At any rate, this stands as one occupation which is a far cry from the ordinary 9-to-5 office job.

TILE DECORATORS add artistic images to ceramic tile and related materials. In some cases, this means using different colored tiles to produce an overall image.

Further Reading

Books

Barry, Bill. *The World of Cartooning: A Complete Guide How to Draw and Sell Cartoons.* CB Publications, 1989.

Butterworth, Emma. *The Complete Book of Calligraphy.* HarperCollins, 1980.

Craig, James. *Graphic Design Career Guide: How to Get a Job and Establish a Career in Design.* Watson-Guptill Publications, 1983.

Dalley, Terrence. *Complete Guide to Illustration and Design.* Book Sales Inc., 1985.

Gautier, Dick. *The Creative Cartoonist.* Putnam Publishing Group, 1989.

Gerberg, Mort. *Cartooning: The Art and Business.* William Morrow, 1989.

Jennings, Simon. *Advanced Illustration and Design.* Book Sales Inc., 1989.

Robinson, Arthur. *Elements of Cartography.* John Wiley, 1984.

Sassoon, Rosemary. *The Practical Guide to Calligraphy.* Thames and Hudson, 1982.

Magazines

Applied Arts
885 Don Mills Road
Toronto, Ontario
M3C 1V9 Canada

Calligraphy Review
1624 24th Avenue, SW
Norman, OK 73072

Greetings
Journal of the Greeting Card and Calendar Association
Haymarket Publishing Ltd.
10-12 The Causeway
Teddington, Middlesex
TW110HE England

How
1507 Dana Avenue
Cincinnati, OH 45207

CHAPTER SEVEN

Odds and Ends

The previous chapters have covered various groups of craft-related careers. Some occupations, however, do not fit readily into any single craft category. Here is a brief overview of some of these additional craft areas, listed in alphabetical order.

Manager

In many craft-related occupations, circumstances can lead to an area of endeavor which differs greatly from craft work itself: management. Becoming a manager may be a step you plan for, or it may be something that just happens. In either case, the prospect of becoming a manager is something every craftsperson should consider.

For example, say you start your own business as a cabinetmaker. Your initial intent is to operate as a one-person shop, and for the first couple of years that is the way you proceed. But as business expands, the need for staff help becomes apparent. So you hire an assistant. Suddenly, you are a manager! This involves all kinds of details which will demand your time and attention. How much should you pay? What tasks should be assigned to the assistant? What hours should be worked? These are fairly simple questions, but they are merely the start of the decision-making process.

Once the employer-employee relationship is established, other questions will arise. How do you motivate the employee to do a good job? What happens if he or she frequently shows up late for work, seems to be sick all the time, or works too slowly? How do you handle a situation in which an employee's mistake ruins a job or in which a customer complains of being treated rudely by your assistant?

We can't provide easy answers to these questions. The point is, unless you operate as a business comprised of a single person, the need to manage people may surface.

Even if you are employed by a small or large business, management opportunities may develop. If you supervise just one part-time worker, you are a manager.

In any management situation, your skill as a craftsperson will be irrelevant. Instead of using your knowledge and manual dexterity to create interesting products, you will be using communication and organization skills to supervise the work of others.

In the eventuality that you find it necessary to take on management responsibilities, follow steps such as these for best success:

- Take classes or seminars in topics such as supervisory skills, basic personnel management, employee motivation, or managing creative people.
- Enroll in a home-study course offered by the American Management Association.
- Read books and magazine articles about management.
- Observe other managers in action and learn from styles and techniques that you find effective.

Although managing people is important, it is not the only type of management. You may also need to develop other types of business and management skills such as business writing and maintaining financial records. Strategies similar to those listed previously can be effective in mastering skills in these areas.

For more information:

American Management Association
135 West 50th Street
New York, NY 10020

Organ Builder

Organ builders pursue a unique, highly specialized craft. Workers in this field build pipe organs or other types of organs, many of them quite large. Typically, the organs they build are used in churches.

Organ builders work with wood, metal, and other materials. Unlike many craft areas, the end result is a single unit which can take months to produce and which may be the work of several people working together.

Most organ builders learn their craft by participating in a formal apprenticeship program sponsored by the American Institute of Organbuilders and the U.S. Department of Labor. This program combines on-the-job training with courses of instruction such as the following:

General Musical Background

Introduction to Organ Building

History of the Organ

General Woodworking

The Organ in its Environment

Metalworking

Technical Design and Execution

Tonal Design

Chest Building

Pipe Making

Wind Systems

Business Administrative Management

Organ Servicing

Language Study (usually German)

Obviously, such a complex list of topics is not to be considered lightly. It takes most people several years to complete an apprenticeship in this field. Those with at least six thousand hours of experience who pass a proficiency exam achieve the status of journeyman. The more advanced status of master organ builder takes at least twelve thousand hours of experience along with other requirements.

Most organ builders work for companies that manufacture organs or other musical instruments. They may specialize in specific areas of organ building. Some focus on repairing rather than building organs, a job which often offers the chance to travel around the United States and Canada.

To be successful, organ builders need patience, tenacity, and skill in working with different materials. A love and understanding of music is also helpful.

The American Institute of Organbuilders includes members from across North America. This group sponsors conventions, seminars, publications, and other opportunities for professional growth.

For more information:

American Institute of Organbuilders
P.O. Box 130982
Houston, TX 77219

Taxidermist

Taxidermists prepare the bodies of fish, birds, mammals, and other animals so that they can be preserved and displayed. Their work includes not just an understanding of basic biology, but also an artistic spirit. In performing their work, taxidermists exercise creativity as they try to make animals look lifelike and interesting. Some taxidermists work for museums. The overall purpose of their job is an educational one, with the emphasis on preserving animals so that they can be displayed for the public. Their jobs may include creating attractive displays of groups of animals as well as preserving individual specimens.

Other taxidermists operate their own businesses, working on a part-time or full-time basis. Primarily, they serve the needs of fishing enthusiasts and hunters who like to display their game as trophies. In addition to prize game fish, deer heads, and small game such as foxes or quail, they may deal with more exotic creatures such as snakes or jungle animals.

Taxidermists generally learn their skills by taking classes or working with experienced professionals. Along with basic techniques of preservation and mounting, they may learn skills ranging from fur processing to creating realistic background displays.

Many working taxidermists belong to the International Guild of Taxidermy. This organization publishes an informative magazine, the *IN-Taxidermist Journal,* which features articles about taxidermy, news from state associations, photos of prize-winning taxidermy work, and other items of interest. Members of the guild enjoy a number of benefits including discounts from supply companies, educational seminars, conventions, and certification programs.

For more information:

International Guild of Taxidermy
P.O. Box 95
South Beloit, IL 61080-0095

Teacher

"Those who can, do. Those who can't, teach."

You have probably heard this old saying before, but don't believe it! This assertion is rarely true in any field, but certainly in crafts it would be virtually impossible to succeed as a teacher without some basic abilities in one or more craft areas. For those with such skills, teaching can provide a way for turning craft-related abilities into a paying job.

Teaching opportunities vary tremendously. They range from part-time or temporary positions teaching a single course or seminar to full-time positions teaching in schools or colleges. Teaching can be done on the side as a way to supplement income from direct work as a craftsperson. It can be a way for those with a job outside of craft areas to keep a hand in their fields of interest. Or it can provide a full-time career.

Teaching possibilities can be found in large cities, smaller towns, and rural areas. For the enterprising crafts practitioner, such opportunities can even be created. This might involve setting up seminars and offering them as an adjunct to a craft business. Or it might mean approaching a school and offering to teach courses that are not presently offered. The continuing education divisions of community colleges, for example, are often receptive to suggestions for new classes. A letter or phone call proposing to teach noncredit classes or seminars in a specific craft area might well lead to teaching assignments.

For teaching jobs with craft schools, submission of a resume and portfolio may be required. A personal interview may also be needed.

For temporary teaching jobs, another option is to present workshops for children in public schools. Check with principals or central office staff to explore such possibilities.

A totally different option is offered by summer camps, which often employ workshop leaders to teach crafts to children. This can be a real change of pace. After all, when was the last time you canoed in the lake at Camp Wichiwoomie? Even if you never attended a summer camp, you probably have a good idea of the typical setting: trees, a lake, counselors, and plenty of activities to entertain boys and girls for a week or more while their parents enjoy a strange and wonderful commodity—silence.

When parents need that break from the kids, somebody has to keep their offspring busy—and that someone could be you. Many summer camps employ instructors to teach a variety of crafts to children. Workshops in pottery, basket making, weaving, craft painting, and many other areas can be quite popular.

To locate jobs in summer camps, take steps such as these:

- Contact the American Camping Association, 12 West 31st Street, New York, NY 10011. Ask for a listing of positions available as craft instructors.
- Check for ads in magazines such as *American Craft* and in newspapers published in areas where camps are located.
- Write to summer camps and ask if any positions are open for the period you have in mind. If you have had previous teaching experience of any kind (even if not related to crafts), be sure to mention it. Also discuss (or list in a resume) your craft competencies.
- Spread the word with friends, teachers, colleagues, or anyone else who might provide a job contact.

Working in a summer camp, as well as other types of teaching, can prove both challenging and beneficial. You can polish teaching skills while practicing your craft, and earn some extra income in the process. Teaching may not be for everyone, but for those with an open mind, it can be fun!

Salesperson

Even if you never actually *make* anything, you can pursue a crafts-related career by selling the materials artisans need to make their products or by marketing completed craft products on behalf of practicing craftspersons. If you are primarily a craftsperson but need to enhance your income, selling craft supplies is also an option.

The market potential for crafts-related supplies is great. In addition to professionals, millions of hobbyists represent potential customers. Schools and colleges also purchase the supplies needed for students in classes and seminars.

One career option in this area is working as a sales representative for a manufacturer. This might involve selling products on a wholesale basis to stores and shops or working directly with the public through telephone sales.

Another possibility is working for a retail store or crafts supplier. Here, you might serve as a clerk, sales associate, or manager. Customers might include professionals, hobbyists, or both.

Still another option is running your own craft supply business. This could be a home-based business or a full-fledged retail store.

In any case, selling to others requires good human relations skills as well as a talent for organization. For the energetic and motivated person, sales work can provide a rewarding alternative or supplement to a crafts career.

For more information:

American Craft Retailers Association
1838 E. 2nd Street
Scotch Plains, NJ 07076

Watermark Association of Artisans
150 Highway 158 East
Camden, NC 27921

U.S. Small Business Administration
1441 L Street, NW
Washington, DC 20416

Further Reading

Audsley, George. *The Art of Organ Building*. Dover Publications (two volumes).

Grantz, Gerald. *Home Book of Taxidermy and Tanning*. Stockpile Books, 1985.

Kelly, Tim. *The Complete Guide to Home Taxidermy*. Meredith Press, 1987.

Kern, Coralee, et al. *How to Run Your Own Home Business*. NTC Publishing Group, 1990.

CHAPTER EIGHT

Breaking In

*I*n our complex society, there are literally thousands of different occupations. Within each job category, however, the number of people actually holding down a paying job may vary tremendously. Certainly, you can't pick up the Sunday newspaper and find thirty classified ads for woodcarver or stained glass maker. On the other hand, people *do* hold jobs carving wood, making stained glass, and pursuing many other craft areas. The question is not whether a crafts career is possible, but how can one get started?

Pursuing a crafts career is similar to going after other types of jobs in some ways, but quite different in others. Here is a brief overview of strategies to follow in getting started. Any one person probably will not need to follow all of these steps but will want to try at least some of them.

Visit Arts and Crafts Fairs

Arts and crafts fairs are common events held frequently around the country, especially during the spring and summer. To get a firsthand look at various crafts, visit such fairs. Stroll around and check out different crafts. Talk to craftspersons about their work. Pay attention to the crowd and see which types of crafts seem most popular with the general public. If you have not yet focused on a particular craft area, use this process to help identify those that seem a good match with your own interests. If you have identified a craft specialty, seek out others in the same area and compare notes.

Read About Crafts

Because crafts are so popular, a great deal of written material is available about them. Chapters 2 through 7 of this book include listings of books on specific crafts and some craft magazines. Use these lists as a starting point in your reading. Visit a local bookstore and pick up a few books. If preferred titles are not available, most stores will order them for you at no extra charge.

A less costly option is consulting a local library. Even small libraries may subscribe to magazines such as *American Craft,* which covers a wide range of craft areas. They should also have books about craft topics and can obtain others through interlibrary loan programs.

Take Craft Classes

As noted throughout this book, classes in different craft areas are common. Enrolling in a class takes you a step farther than reading or visiting craft fairs, for the student's role provides actual hands-on experience. This not only teaches you fundamental skills, but also helps you determine whether a given craft area is right for you. It's one thing to read about making pottery, for instance, but quite another to do it.

Craft classes vary immensely in scope, setting, and price. Some of those presented as summer seminars, for example, are rather expensive. Others, such as those offered through community colleges, can be quite reasonable.

Unless you are interested in a full-fledged degree or diploma program, you need not worry about tests, final grades, or similar concerns. Most craft classes are offered on a noncredit basis without exams or grading.

Just some of the sponsors of craft classes include the following:

- Arts and crafts schools
- Community, junior, and technical colleges
- Trade schools or "career colleges"
- Extension or continuing education divisions of four-year colleges and universities
- Public school districts with adult and community education programs
- County or city recreation departments
- Churches, YMCAs, or other community organizations
- Practicing craftspersons who offer their own lessons or classes

To find out about classes or workshops, contact schools and ask for a catalog or schedule of classes. Most schools are glad to provide publications and will furnish all the information you need.

Experiment with Different Crafts

Unless you have already committed to a single craft area, try out several craft areas before settling on a given specialty. This might consist of taking classes or simply obtaining the necessary materials and completing a basic project or two. The approach here may be closer to that of the craft hobbyist than the craft professional, but a little diversity never hurts. Who knows? You might discover a flair for a craft you never previously considered. Conversely, you might find that a craft which seemed appealing is not that enjoyable to you after all, and save yourself a considerable investment of time and money.

Learn from the Experts

In the Middle Ages and much more recently, the only way to learn a craft was to serve as an apprentice to an accomplished craftsperson. This was a long, involved, and highly structured process, but it paid off. Today, formal apprenticeships are less common, but you can utilize a variation of the process to break into the craft area of your choice.

At its simplest level, this might consist simply of visiting practicing craftspersons and asking questions about their work. Ask about special techniques, sources of raw materials, how their work is selling, problems they have encountered, where they buy equipment, and so forth.

For a more intensive experience, offer to serve as a part-time assistant. Be willing to work on an unpaid basis if necessary, with the chance to learn about the craft in lieu of payment. If the craftsperson is highly successful, a paying job might be a possibility. In either case, the main objective is to learn as much about the business as possible.

Develop Credentials

If you are selling work at an arts and crafts fair, the work will generally stand on its own. Your own background may not be relevant.

In some cases, though, you may need to market not only your work, but also yourself. For example, a potential customer may want to commission you to take on a project or a school might consider you to teach a class. In these and other instances, having related credentials will be important.

There are many ways to develop credentials. In addition to work experience, here are some of them:

- Complete a degree or diploma program.
- Complete an apprenticeship.
- Participate in seminars or short courses.

- Become certified by a craft organization.
- Compete in contests and win awards.
- Present talks, workshops, or seminars.

Any of these steps can show others that you have special skills or knowledge—the real purpose of credentials. Once you earn credentials, don't be shy about sharing them. Letting others know of special credentials is not bragging, but just good business. If you earn certificates or diplomas, display them. List credentials in resumes, brochures about you and your work, bio sheets, or other outlets. The more such information is distributed, the more successful you appear to others.

Also, consider developing a portfolio of your work. Samples (or photos of samples) of your work can serve as visual confirmation of your special skills.

Join Professional Organizations

One of the best ways to expand your horizons as a craftsperson is to join one or more professional organizations. These groups can be helpful in getting your career started as well as in keeping it going. Through networking, sharing information, and a variety of other services, these groups provide important help to craftspersons.

Previous chapters of this book have listed various groups related to specific craft areas. A more general group is the American Craft Council. This national group fosters interests in crafts and provides a wide range of services to members.

If you join a professional organization, be active in its activities. Stay in touch with other members, and attend conventions, seminars, or other meetings if possible.

For more information:

American Craft Council
P.O. Box 3000
Danville, NJ 07834-9805

Take the First Step

Whatever strategies you choose in pursuing a crafts career, the most important move is taking the first step. (Actually, you could consider reading this book the first step; in that case, it's your *next* step that really counts!) If working in a craft area seems appealing, move from the mode of *thinking* about it to *doing* it.

Too risky? Then minimize the risk. Start small. Be a part-time craftsperson. Invest a little time and perhaps a small amount of money. Then if you enjoy the experience, expand the scope of your activities.

The Future for Crafty People

When one looks ahead to the remainder of the 1990s and on into the twenty-first century, the future looks bright for persons working in various craft areas. This is not empty optimism, but is a prediction based on factors such as these:

The continued advance of technology will make handcrafted products seem even more special.

Nostalgia for the past will help keep many craft areas popular.

While recessions may come and go, the number of people with discretionary income will continue to be large. There will be many people who are not only interested in craft products, but able to afford them. This should be particularly true of the Baby Boom generation as it ages.

The increasing level of international trade and travel should be a boon to craft producers and sellers. American arts and crafts are already popular in many nations, and this popularity should increase as more foreign tourists travel to North America and as trade between nations grows.

Crafts do have a bright future. The only question remaining is this: Will you be a part of that future? Here's hoping the answer is a firm and optimistic *yes*.